Praise for Dean Lindsay and Cracking the Networking CODE

See cover for endorsements from Brian Tracy, Ken Blanchard, Frank Bracken, Ginger Benedict, and Bill Brooks.

"Dean Lindsay's easy-to-read *Cracking the Networking CODE* is filled with fresh insights and practical tips on how to build meaningful, win-win relationships for your business and your life."

> *-- Gary Keller*
> *Best-selling author of* The Millionaire Real Estate Agent

"*Cracking the Networking CODE* cracked me up for all the right reasons. This book is tight, succinct, and full of wit. Dean Lindsay is one sharp and funny guy. I have been in the corporate arena for over forty years and we have needed Dean Lindsay's unique voice for far too long. He makes common sense into common practice. Great book. Great message. Great reading. Enjoy."

> *-- Max Derden*
> *Partner, PricewaterhouseCoopers LLP*

"Dean Lindsay makes it fun to become a good networker, a 'progress agent' as he says. This book is a hip, fun, easy read that is filled with specific tips for connecting and staying connected with others. It is also filled with enough trivia and 'significa' to give you even more to talk about. Read, laugh, learn, and improve."

> *-- Jim Cathcart*
> *Author of* Relationship Selling

"I wish I had this book when I was starting my consulting business. This book will knock five years off your learning curve."

> *-- Vince Poscente*
> *Olympic speed skier*
> *Author of* The Ant and the Elephant: Leadership for the Self

"For over three years, our entire sales team has benefited from Dean sharing his topnotch business-building insights – insights now found in his smart, engaging, and powerful *Cracking the Networking CODE*. While utilizing Dean's fresh insights, along with his personal coaching and mentoring, our sales professionals have taken their success to the next level! Live this book. *Be Progress*."

> *– J. Lee Ripley*
> *Field Vice President*
> *Pacific Life & Annuity Company*

"Dean Lindsay writes on the subject of networking and relationship building with conviction and authority. His writing, *Cracking the Networking CODE*, will be of immense and immediate value to anyone aiming for greater effectiveness in marketing and selling."

> *-- Jack Kinder, Jr. and Garry D. Kinder*
> *Speakers, authors, consultants*

Praise for Dean Lindsay and Cracking the Networking CODE

"What a fantastic read on the ABC's of networking. This page turner provides a very clear and concise system that will allow anyone, even the most introverted, to become a progress agent. "
-- *Steve Wentz*
Vice President, CB Richard Ellis

"This is a great book, simply written and easily readable, that will definitely help you meet, connect, and develop long-term relationships with others. A must read for anyone who has to deal with people."
-- *Dr. Tony Alessandra*
Author of The Platinum Rule *and* Charisma

"Whether you are looking for a new job or thinking about changing careers, *Cracking the Networking CODE* is the book for you. It reveals what the human resource community has known and kept secret for years. Networking is the key to unlock the door to any position and this book gives you the combination to that lock."
-- *Gayle Ciupak*
Manager, Human Resources, General Motors

"A terrific book that'll show you how to build and nurture profitable relational capital. A keeper." -- *Nido R. Qubein*
Chairman, Great Harvest Bread Company
Founder, National Speakers Association Foundation

"*Cracking the networking CODE* is a terrific resource for anyone who is in the business of meeting people. This book clarifies how to maximize networking opportunities." -- *Harry LaRosiliere, CFP*
First Vice President-Investments, Morgan Stanley

"What an important book! I have never seen anything like this in Sweden. Highly informative yet extremely entertaining, this is a book I would give to all my colleagues. It's perfect for any professional wanting to make his or her way in today's global business environment. An easy read – and a must read!"
-- *Jonas Milton (Stockholm, Sweden)*
President (VD) of Almega

"Effective networking has locks that must be opened to create long-lasting business. Dean's CODE is the set of keys you need to open those locks! Don't just read this book – study and apply it to achieve success. I love it!"
-- *Stephanie Saunders Ahlberg*
Top-producing San Francisco Real Estate Broker
Author of the How May I Serve You? *business column*

Praise for Dean Lindsay and Cracking the Networking CODE

"Dean Lindsay has redefined networking from the mindless, self-serving distribution of business cards to a connecting, collaborative, communicative process. Reading this book is an absolute necessity in today's changing environment."
-- Helen Harkness, Ph.D.
Founder, Career Design Associates, Inc.
Author of Capitalizing on Career Chaos

"We *present* to our network every day…Let Dean's powerful message on this subject help you grow your relationships."
-- Tony Jeary, Mr. Presentation™
Author of Life Is a Series of Presentations

"Read this book ONLY if you plan to take action. Definitely not 'shelf-ware,' this book is chock-full of tips and tidbits – real, honest-to-goodness specifics wrapped around the CORE principles. Build or expand your network of relationships with this fun guide. Of course, making them pay off is the hard part – but Deano makes it completely doable."
-- Dianna Booher
Author of Communicate with Confidence,
From Contact to Contract, *and* Your Signature Work

"Dean is energetic, passionate, and committed to success. If you read his book, you just might learn his secret." *-- Joel Zeff*
National speaker and humorist

"Dean Lindsay has taken an often misunderstood subject and turned it into a helpful resource for the reader. Anyone who wants to increase their business skills must first better understand the importance of people skills. This book is a must read in order to accomplish that objective."
-- Dr. Robert A. Rohm
President, Personality Insights, Inc.
Author of Positive Personality Profiles

"Every once in a while a GREAT book comes to my desk, and how I love it! Such a book is *Cracking the Networking CODE* by Dean Lindsay.
I especially like the words in the title which make up the CODE, and his genius ideas about creating personal 'Curb Appeal.' You will want to buy a case – or several cases – of this great new book to give to your family and best clients. It is a true treasure!" *-- Dottie Walters, CSP*
Author of Speak and Grow Rich
President, Walters International Speakers Bureau

Praise for Dean Lindsay and Cracking the Networking CODE

"Wow! Dean Lindsay has hit a home run with his book, *Cracking the Networking CODE*! This is the best networking book I have read in a long time! I believe that networking is the best single factor in building a business, and Dean has written a book in a clear and concise manner that is fun to read, and that pinpoints the importance of networking effectively! This is sure to be a bestseller!"

> *-- Jana L. High*
> *Author of* High-Tech Etiquette
> *Coauthor of* The Princess Principle
> *and* The Service Path

"Dean Lindsay not only gives some great advice on networking in this easy-to-read book, but he also provides the 'why bother.' Make sure you don't miss the pearls of wisdom as you are being entertained by the ways he expresses his ideas."

> *-- Al Lucia*
> *Author of* A Slice of Life *and*
> JukeBox Journey to Success

"*Cracking the Networking CODE* breaks down the networking process into easy, understandable steps, with the emphasis on creating long-term, caring, giving relationships. Dean Lindsay is teaching an important life need, not just a business skill."

> *-- Ross K. Bennett*
> *Founder/President*
> *Red Pepper Productions, Inc.*

"If you want to take the pain out of networking and get the results you want, you must read this book. It's a delightful way to connect with others to grow your business."

> *-- Maura Schreier-Fleming*
> *Author of* Real-World Selling for
> Out-of-This-World Results

"As the ancient Chinese saying goes...'Lazy man must wait long time for roast duck to fly into mouth.' Dean's tasty insights will help you place successful orders for life's greatest rewards."

> *-- Ken Bradford*
> *Author of* Fearless & Persuasive Speaking

Cracking the Networking CODE

A Progress Agent's Guide to

Cracking the Networking CODE

4 Steps to Priceless Business Relationships

Dean Lindsay
Progress Agent ™

Second Edition 2005

ISBN 0-9761141-0-0

LCCN 2004096683

ATTENTION CORPORATIONS, UNIVERSITIES, COLLEGES, AND PROFESSIONAL ORGANIZATIONS:

Quantity discounts are available on bulk purchases of this book for educational,
gift purposes, or as premiums for increasing magazine subscriptions or renewals.
Special books or book excerpts can also be created to fit specific needs.

**For more information, please contact World Gumbo Publishing
toll-free at 1-888-318-2911 or e-mail us at info@WorldGumbo.com.
www.WorldGumbo.com**

To Lena, Sofia, and Ella

Acknowledgments

Special Thanks to:

Doug Barkley, Jo-Ann Langseth, Dr. Bob Rich, Cindy Peters, Kelley Akins, Robin Creasman, Carl Youngberg, Scott Hasse, Larry Becker, Lee Ripley, Jan Morgan, Jerry Lindsay, Marilyn and Tom Ross, Amy Dunker, Joel Zeff, Jack Teschemacher, David Strutton, Sandy Hayes, Vince Poscente, Jana High, Lance Lindsay, Paul Rosowski, Lisa Ferrari, Jürgen Mahneke and the team at the Bavarian Grill, George Hendley, Dale Turner, Stefan Stenberg, Betty Garrett, Irene Kohlman, Anita Vanetti, Jonas Bond, Andra Grava, Noel Mares, Anne Sadovsky, Eddie Coker, Henry Gentry, David Lindsey, Mark Langford, Jim Young, Gloria Daniel, Jeff Rhoades, Jeff Edwards, Brooke Hopkins, JS Covington, Martha Malnor, Sammy Gardner, Vicki Motsinger, Shirley Tillinghast, Martha Lawrence, Cindy McHenry, Jay Papasan, Bonnie Joyce, and to all the fine authors and business professionals who endorsed this project.

Extra Special Thanks to Jay Conrad Levinson. Having you, a true marketing guru, write the foreword to my first book is almost beyond belief. Way cool, Jay.

Credits:

Editor: Jo-Ann Langseth – Warwick, Rhode Island
Editorial Insight: Dr. Bob Rich – Healesville, Victoria (Australia)
Index: Martha Malnor – Katy, Texas
Cover Photo: JS Covington – Irving, Texas
Cover Layout: Noel Mares / The Trade Group – Carrollton, Texas
Book Manufacturing: Thomson-Shore, Inc. – Dexter, Michigan

> Code – 1. *A system of rules, regulations, principles or laws on any subject setting a standard.* 2. *A system of symbols or signals providing a means of communication used for transmitting messages.*

Contents

Foreword By
Jay Conrad Levinson
The Father of Guerrilla Marketing

Dean Lindsay is a master of progress, and in this book will show you how to be the same. He'll take you by the hand – a pleasurable experience, because the man is an awesome writer – and lead you into the land of networking nirvana.

In that land of networking, you'll need no <u>net</u> because you'll have the confidence and ability to be a gold-medal networker, and you'll realize that superb networking is not a lot of <u>work</u> – if you do it right. And within these pages is where you'll learn to do it right.

Your guide and shepherd will be Dean's Code. There really is a code. And it's the real deal – a way for you to make networking your most powerful marketing tool. I know a thing or three about marketing, and I know that networking is an exceptionally effective, economical, and rewarding marketing tactic.

Lots of people do it. Very few of them do it right. Read this remarkably easy-to-read book, act upon what you learn, and you'll do it right every time. You'll look forward to networking because you'll have reaped many of its rewards, because you'll have mastered its intricacies, and because you'll know you'll have fun at the networking function – be it a black-tie dinner or a trade show.

Dean Lindsay has the ability to take a complex and very misunderstood topic, and make it primer simple and crystal clear. Dare I say that he also makes it easy to do? *Yes, I dare.*

You are a lucky reader. You're about to learn how you can stand for progress in the minds of people who are privileged to meet you – and believe me, they will feel privileged. You're about to tap into universal truths that will change your perspective, your attitudes, and especially your net worth.

You're going to learn exactly what networking is not, and probably feel guilty for not having comprehended its possibilities till now. But as we all know, now is the first day of the rest of your life. And now, you're about to crack the networking code.

That's going to make a huge difference in your life. I'm honored that Dean has asked me to usher you into the treasures of networking.

I glow with the bright promise this book offers to you, and I glow at how it will illuminate and enrich the lives of the people who meet you.

Jay Conrad Levinson
Marin County, California
The Father of Guerrilla Marketing
Author, "Guerrilla Marketing" series of books
Over 14 million sold; now in 41 languages
www.gmarketing.com

From Dean

A Guarantee:

If you master the CODE and consistently utilize the strategies and tips found in this book, you WILL build priceless business relationships. *I guarantee it.*

But first you must act on the stuff in here. Learning 'HOW' to build priceless business relationships through networking is NOT the goal. Actually, BUILDING priceless business relationships through networking is the goal.

Learning should not lead to simply knowing.
Learning should lead to ACTION.

A Warning:

This is *not* a textbook.
We are going to have some fun along the way.

Let's get cracking.

Net-Work-Ing

Come on. Jump in.
The Water's Fine.

When I was growing up, my grandparents *(Tom and Jerry Courtney of Shreveport, Louisiana – yes, Tom and Jerry. Cool, huh?)* would treat the entire family to a long Labor Day weekend at the Island Cottages in Hot Springs, Arkansas.

The highlight of the trip *(besides eating Aunt Toe's homemade brownies while watching the Jerry Lewis Telethon and a shopping spree at K-Mart)* was when all of us piled into Gran Gran and Dan Dan's mid '70s Tri Sonic modified V ski boat for an hour-long boat ride to the dam between Lake Hamilton and Lake Ouachita. The trip should have taken only about 25 minutes but there were 14 life-vested sardines crammed into a boat built for eight.

The water that came out of this dam was super cold because it came from the very bottom of Lake Ouachita. It was so cold that the air temperature would plummet as you neared the dam. When we got there we would have a competition to see which of us cousins would be the first to jump in, and then who could stay underwater the longest, and then who could swim the most laps around the boat without turning into an ice cube.

At first, we would just stick our toes into the water, then our feet, before someone would finally jump in or *get pushed in.* The first one in would try to get the rest of us to jump in by acting like it wasn't that cold and saying stuff like, *"Come on. Jump in. The water's fine."* We knew it was cold but we also knew it was FUN. So finally we would all jump in and the contests would be on. The water was uncomfortable at first but gradually we would get used to it.

By the end of the afternoon it was always hard to get us back in the boat, because we were having such a great time and none of the adults were willing to jump in and get us out.

For many, networking is a lot like going swimming in ice-cold water. They would prefer to dip their toes in and wade around a bit before going further. That is understandable. However, to really harness the power of networking, you are going to have to jump in and swim around.

It might be tough at first. You can do it. Do what is uncomfortable until it becomes comfortable and you will never stop. Come on. Jump in. The water's fine.

Please consider this book a push.

From Met to Net

There is this unassuming little word you always find in the biographies of famous people. The word is "met."

Then William R. Hewlett met David Packard.
Then Dean Martin met Jerry Lewis.
Then Sid met Nancy.
Then Siegfried met Roy.

We meet people all the time. Meeting people is part of life. Meeting people is one of the fundamental steps of networking.

So why is meeting new people in a networking situation so intimidating?
Why is it so tough?
How do some people make it look so easy?
What is their secret?

Again, we *meet* people all the time. They are everywhere. Meeting people may be necessary in successful networking, but it is not the only step. There is a big difference between meeting someone and building a priceless business relationship with them.

How do you build a powerful personal network?

This is an important question to consider because, to a large degree, who you know and associate with determines who you become in life.

"We think of ourselves as individuals,
but we are embedded in networks of relationships
that define and sustain us."
-- Michael Nichols

The most successful, well-rounded and happy people are most often the ones who are best connected to other successful, well-rounded and happy people. When these people need support or information, they know the right people to call.

How well-connected you are determines your access to those with the most money, the best contacts, the real power and influence *(not to mention the best seats at sporting events)*. Being connected to the right people opens up opportunities for you and your company.

> **"A noble person attracts noble people and knows how to hold onto them."**
> *-- Johann Wolfgang von Goethe*

Building solid relationships with other professionals in your field is also a crucial part of career development and job-hunting. During tough economic times, your network has the power to help you make a positive move and provide a stepping stone to your next career. Best to develop your network before you need it.

If you are already looking for a new job, deep down in your blood pumper you already know that you need to get out there and connect with people. Sure, in a perfect world, your track record and past successes would speak for themselves, but without professional and personal contacts, your two-page spiffy resume on off-white professional-grade paper is likely going to just take up space in a pile on a hiring manager's overstimulated desk.

You are going to have to log off Monster, move away from the keyboard, and find a room to work.

For many professionals, successful networking is something of an enigma because the skills needed to network successfully are simple to understand but not necessarily easy to consistently implement. Networking is an art as well as a skill. Take the time to develop the art of networking.

Networking is a creative process. You are creating ways to serve and to help people progress. You progress when you help others progress. Each of us has wonderfully unique gifts to share with others.

> **"The final frontier may be human relationships, one person to another."**
> *-- Buzz Aldrin*

When you have made someone feel good, helped them progress or solve a problem, they talk about you in a good way to all the people who are in their network. You create a positive word-of-mouth, a positive buzz. You are worthy of buzz. You are buzzworthy. Keep doing this and your buzzworthiness grows.

Buzzworthiness?

Is that even a word?

Top Ten Benefits of Networking

As William Allman, the author of *Stone Age Present,* states, "The key to our species' success is our great skill in making close alliances with others." *True enough.* There are many benefits to harnessing the power of networking and *Cracking the Networking CODE.* **Here are the Top Ten:**

1. Friendship and support

2. Advice and access to different points of view

3. New career paths, employment, and business opportunities

4. Referrals and introductions to professionals and quality prospects

5. Important information (Market/organizational shifts, upcoming events, etc.)

6. Promotions or lateral moves within your organization

7. Unique sales ideas from sales professionals in other fields

8. Introductions to quality vendors and resources

9. Advocates within related organizations and industries

10. More sales

> **"You have to accept that no matter where you work, you are not an employee; you are in a business with one employee – yourself."**
> *- Andrew S. Grove*

Networking's Bum Rap

Unfortunately, the term "networking" has gotten a bum rap. I have consistently asked professionals I am working with to share with me what they think of when they hear the word 'networking.' Far too often I hear it conjures up images of manipulative, self-serving, insincere and predatory individuals, who are on the prowl for someone they can pounce on, try to sell something to, or solicit an unearned favor from.

When meeting someone new, ineffective networkers will rapidly scan new acquaintances to prejudge their usefulness while regurgitating their blanket sales pitch and robotically handing out their business card before abruptly moving on to their next victim. This is a waste of time for the ineffective networker and the unfortunate people they corner.

Here is an actual conversation I had with an ineffective networker.

Me: *Tell me about the networking event yesterday.*

Ineffective Networker: *I did great. I handed out 35 cards.*

Me: *Did you strike up some good conversations?*

Ineffective Networker: *What? I was busy. I handed out 35 cards.*

Me: *OK. How many cards did you get?*

Ineffective Networker: *Ah, I think two.*

Savvy networkers judge their success not by how many cards they give out, but by how many they have collected and the relationships they have potentially created. After connecting with someone and getting their business card, reconnecting with them is paramount.

Networking can be a lifelong skill that allows shortcuts to important people and information. Anything is possible through networking. It should make life easier. The key is to cultivate relationships by sharing ideas, information, and resources. Work to set up "win-win" situations where all parties benefit from the exchange, whether immediately or sometime in the future.

Networking is NOT forcing yourself or your products on someone. Networking IS getting to know people, their lives, and their needs. Networking is NOT selling your products and services. Networking IS selling yourself.

Successful networking saves time and money while reducing frustration. Everyone networks. Every professional, in every type of career and in every aspect of commerce, networks. Every occupation has networking opportunities. Dentists, plumbers, and taxidermists each have their yearly meeting of some type where they come together to chew the industry fat.

Networking is nothing new. Most of our relationships began through networking and referrals. Heck, *Paul McCartney met John Lennon through networking.* Networking is simply two or more parties meeting for mutual benefit.

It is natural to want to share, help, give, and contribute.

Successful Networking
= Being Progress

To be successful in today's world, you need great business relationships. To build those great relationships, you need to help others be successful. You need to help them progress.

Everyone connects with others with the goal of progressing in some way. You need to be seen as an agent for their progress, a catalyst for them to take a positive step forward. They need to feel that you make a positive impact on their life, that you bring value. It's amazing how many people lose sight of this fundamental dynamic.

Everything we do, consciously or subconsciously, we do because we believe the perceived consequences of those actions will bring us what I label the Six Ps of Progress.

The Six Ps of Progress:	**Pleasure**
	Peace of Mind
	Profit
	Prestige
	Pain Avoidance
	Power™

This goes for eating, shopping, exercising, hugging, crying, working, going to the movies – whatever. Each of us makes decisions as to what to read, who to talk to, what to buy, where to eat, what to eat, who to take phone calls from, and who to help, based on whether we think these acts will bring us these *Six Ps of Progress* ™.

At each moment, we make decisions based on what we *think* will bring these benefits – short-term or long-term. It has long been the first principle of marketing to answer this unasked question.

At a mostly subconscious level, we are continuously thinking to ourselves:

Is taking this action (talking with this person, etc.) helping me move toward pleasure, peace of mind, profit, prestige, power, or helping me to avoid pain? <u>*Is this action Progress, or is it simply change?*</u>

The people we meet must view being around us as **progress, not change.** *It is natural to resist change but we embrace progress.* All progress is change but not all change is progress. Change is inevitable, progress is a choice. Building a relationship with us must be viewed as progress if we hope others will choose to alter their lives to include us.

You need to constantly look for ways to help people progress. You need to *Be Progress* ™ in their eyes. You must be seen as a catalyst for their progress, an agent in their progress. You need to be a *Progress Agent* ™. When you meet new people, make your number-one priority finding ways to help that person move toward the *Six Ps of Progress* ™.

The most successful individuals in any industry are those who become Progress Agents – and stay Progress Agents. They help people. They share information. They maintain their visibility and credibility. They show they care. They're authentic – the real thing! They consistently say and do the things that are necessary to demonstrate that they're in the relationship for the long term.

Make sure you are always making positive progress-based impressions. People need to be aware of you in a positive way. People must *be aware* of you, not *beware* of you.

It's really not that tough. Most people on the planet get pleasure when people smile at them, listen to them, and take interest in what they say. Pleasure is Progress. So that's a pretty safe place to start.

Are You a Progress Agent™?

Before we go any further, answer this question:

Do I genuinely want to understand and help fulfill the needs of others?

If you do – *good.* You have the makings of a Progress Agent ™ as well as an effective networker. A nurturing, giving attitude is the cornerstone to *Cracking the Networking CODE.*

If you don't – you are going to have a tough time making networking work for you. But there is still hope…Read on!

All effective networkers help others to progress. Networking is not a one-way street. It's more like an eight-lane superhighway speeding in both directions – both people need to benefit. Networking is reciprocal.

When making new acquaintances, many people unwisely focus *only* on their own personal gain. It is far wiser to learn to appreciate the other person and learn what you can do to be supportive. Relationships need nurturing.

Again, start with a smile.
Sounds simple, and it is, very simple. People like people who smile at them. It makes them smile back and smiling brings pleasure. If you smile when you first see someone, it helps them feel good and that is a solid start.

> **"Stick your teeth in the air.**
> **Show the world you care."**
> *-- Eddie Coker*

Give before you receive.
Successful networkers know they must contribute befo re they can
expect a return on their investment. Try to match and connect the
knowledge, skills, and sensibilities of the various people you meet
with others you have already established relationships with.

Give a smile - Get a smile.
Give help - Get help.
Introduce people to people - People introduce people to you.
Care - Get cared for.
Listen - Get listened t o.
Help others progress - Progress.
Give referrals - Get referrals.

Ask yourself:

Do people perceive me as a generous helper or more as a selfish
taker?

Careful here. If you wear the *selfish taker* label, people will
eventually whittle you out of their loop. This is exactly the opposite
outcome you are looking for.

> **"You get the best out of others when**
> **you give the best of yourself."**
> *-- Harry Firestone*

Start today. Say it loud. Say it proud.

I like to help.
Today I am going to help and give – and then help and give
some more.

Become a Progress Agent ™.

Networking: The Way Around the "Do Not Call" List

Wow. Cold-calling over the phone is tough. Most sales professionals find it taxing and most consumers don't like it much either.

Think about it. *Do you like to be cold-called? Does it work on you?*

Cold Caller: *Mr. Jun..dson?*

Mr. Johnson: *That's Johnson.*

Cold Caller: *Oh… (giggle) sorry. Is Mr. Johnson there?*

Mr. Johnson: *No. (Click.)*

Consumers dislike being solicited by phone so much that a law was passed enabling them to get their names on a "Do Not Call" list. A whole bunch of people – 62 million, and counting! – got themselves on that list as soon as they could. *Maybe even you. I know I did.*

These consumers invested the time to get on this list to say a big, fat ***"NO thank you! Please do not call me."***

Now some companies are trying to find legal ways to keep phoning them up, sometimes even eating up consumers' cell phone minutes.

What is up with that? Why call someone who has already told you they do NOT want you to call?

29

The Do Not Call list is a HUGE hint that these people do not like cold calls.

They do not like them in the morning.
They do not like them while they're snoring.
They do not like them while watching TV.
Not even 'courtesy calls' from AT&T.
They do not like them about how to invest,
Or how to save more than all the rest.
They would not like them with a special rate.
They would not like them with an expiration date.
Not with a special offer,
Not from a hacking cougher.
They do not like this telephone Spam.
They do not like it, Spam I am.   — *Thank you, Dr. Seuss.*

A solid and gracious way around the Do Not Call list is to get out and meet people. You can earn a fortune – *and have some fun in the process* – building relationships with quality business professionals through networking. Networking sets you apart from the 'smile and dial' boiler-room sales types who interrupt people's dinner hour with their pitches. Think of networking as drawing on shared interests to create and encourage mutually favorable relationships. It is the back-scratch boogie.

Don't have the time?
Make the time. In today's competitive environment, networking is a practical and valuable tool that no individual in business can live without.

Harness the Power in Numbers

There is power in numbers. When you effectively build relationships with others, you have the opportunity to reach many more people than you could ever reach on your own. After a while, your networking "web" will interconnect and seem to go on and on, even when you're not working at it heavily. Connections will continuously be made.

Do not underestimate the power of your contact. It is well documented that most people have some form of relationship with around 250 people *(widely referred to as their Circle of Influence)*. These are not 250 people they would invite to their Christmas – Hanukkah – or even Festivus party *(just a little something for the Seinfeld fans)*.

These are 250 people they know directly or indirectly, ranging from family members to random contacts that involve some amount of persuasion. This persuasion is used all the time to recommend a good restaurant, shoe store, plastic surgeon, energy drink, personal trainer, handyman, florist or _____*(insert your profession here)*.

Theoretically, each of your 250-some-odd contacts *could* recommend you and your services to 250 additional people. *That is cool to think about and empowering to consider!*

But here's the rub:
Just because they COULD recommend you, your products, and your services to 250 others does not mean that they ARE or that they WILL.

Some quick questions to ask yourself:

Do people have a trusting impression of me and my services? Why, or why not?

Do they see me, my company, and my services as providing progress?

Do they value what I do for them and others?

Enough to recommend me to others?

Enough to use my service themselves?

Do they value their relationship with me?

Do they feel that a relationship with me means progress for them?

It comes down to trust and value.

How do we build trust? How do we establish value?

Trust is a feeling. It is a buzz. Trust is fluid. It is fragile. Value is established in the mind of the beholder. Trust between people is built moment by moment, year to year. Value is established over time.

It takes a series of positive impressions. Think about the people you trust. *Why do you trust them?*

Is it because they said *"Trust me"* or *"You can trust me"*?

No, these people have proven themselves trustworthy by continually doing things in a way that has built our trust. They got to know us. They care about us. They are reliable.

In short, they earned our trust by "giving a hoot." Few people *give a hoot* these days. When you show genuine interest in others, it shines a big attractive spotlight on you as someone with whom to cultivate a relationship. We have all met people who are totally focused on themselves, their interests, and their goals.

Are they fun to talk to?

Can you rely on them?

Are they people you want to help?

It is, of course, vital to know where you want to go in life. But if you exclude others because of your self-absorption, you are actually slowing down your own progress. Include others in your journey. Work hard not to be egotistical or selfish. Work diligently to increase the number of people you actively support and who support you.

Helping others to progress is the proverbial two-sided coin. It helps you to progress in equal measure.

> **"One of the most beautiful compensations of this life is that no one can sincerely try to help another without helping himself."**
> *-- Ralph Waldo Emerson*

Gaining Confidence:
Talking to Strangers

Networking requires assertiveness. Some people find it easy to strike up conversations with strangers and keep track of old colleagues. For others, networking is a tough, mysterious, and largely neglected process. Be a conversation starter. Talk to everyone, everywhere! For most people, learning how to meet and talk with strangers isn't easy. But do not ignore strangers.

I know what your parents said,
but you must talk to strangers.

A coaching client of mine had been trying for months to get a certain businessman to join him at a very active weekly networking event sponsored by his local Chamber of Commerce. Finally this gentleman visited the event.

He walked into the room packed with people. He looked at the pool of business professionals. Looked at my client and said, *"I don't know anyone at this thing. I'm out of here!"* And he LEFT, literally turning his back on a roomful of opportunities.

When my client told me about his misguided friend, it reminded me of the classic story of the two sales professionals who were sent to sell shoes to the Aborigines.

One sends a telegram back to headquarters reading,
"No opportunities here. No one is wearing shoes."

The other sends a telegram back that says,
"Plenty of opportunities here. No one is wearing shoes!"

But be careful: you can go to a networking event and not have any networking moments. I define a 'networking moment' as a true connection -- not just meeting someone. The art of networking is not in meeting people. The art is in connecting with people.

It is all in how you look at it. You have to see strangers for what they are – opportunities to *Be Progress* ™. Plus, when you talk to strangers they stop being strangers. *They might still seem strange, but they're no longer strangers.*

At one point:
Bill Gates and Paul Allen were strangers.
You and your significant other were strangers.
Miles Davis and Charlie Parker were strangers.
Keith and Mick were strangers.
Oprah and Dr. Phil were strangers.
Nick and Jessica were strangers.
Sonny and Cher were strangers.
Those Google dudes were strangers.

Also, it is safe to assume that most people are at least a tad nervous at networking functions. Help others get more comfortable by approaching them first. It is boring and close to a waste of time to attend a networking function and just stand around waiting for someone to come up to you and inquire about what you sell, or ask for your card. Effective networking involves more than just showering and showing up.

> **"Behold the turtle. He makes progress only when he sticks his neck out."**
> *-- James B. Conant*

Commit yourself to proactively meeting and connecting with new people. Find common interests. Be open to new ideas and opportunities. Scope out ways to help. Be Progress ™.

The CODE Revealed

No doubt you've been wondering, "When is Deano going to get to the CODE?" Well, here it is, the CODE revealed. *Drum roll, please.*

The four letters that make up the word CODE stand for the four steps consistently taken by the most effective networkers to crack the networking CODE and start building priceless business relationships. Effective networkers:

C: *Create Personal Curb Appeal*

Effective networkers feel successful and display a genuine desire to help others progress. They look and act the part of someone you would want to have in your corner.

O: *Open Face-to-Face Relationships*

Effective networkers research the various networking options and commit to a nctworking strategy. They get out and about and reach out. They open relationships.

D: *Deliver Solid First Impressions*

Effective networkers know their first impression sets the foundation for all future impressions, and they make sure it's a good one.

E: *Earn Trust*

Effective networkers follow up and keep in touch. They stay involved with the people they meet and earn their trust through a series of progress-based impressions. They continually find ways to help. *This is where most ineffective networkers drop the ball.*

The remainder of this book will delve into each of these four steps to *Cracking the Networking CODE*.

Step 1

C - Create Personal Curb Appeal

Be a Success in Your Own Eyes

The first step in *Cracking the Networking CODE* is to:
Create Personal Curb Appeal.

Most people connect the term "curb appeal" to checking out a house or building from the street. *How does it look from the street? Is it attractive to the eye from the outside?*

Personal curb appeal involves much more than how you look on the outside. Sure, you need to look sharp when networking, but **real personal curb appeal originates from within**. Before you even start networking, you must feel it is inevitable that you will meet and help people. You must feel it is inevitable that you will continue to progress. It simply will happen. It is happening. You will help other people reach their goals. You will reach your goals. You are progressing and you help others progress.

People pick up on that feeling. It's a buzz, an aura. It surrounds you. It's appealing. It draws the right people to you. Andra Grava, an extremely well-connected business owner and entrepreneur in my network, told me about a really interesting networking group called *Success North Dallas*. One of their few criteria for membership is that you must *be a success in your own eyes.*

Be a success in your own eyes. That's what I'm talking about. You have to feel successful. Not Cocky or Uppity, just good about yourself. This creates personal curb appeal. You can't go to a networking event looking for success. You have to take success with you to the event. Success breeds success. Success attracts success.

It is so important to feel successful, to feel like a winner. Feeling successful makes you PHAT. PHAT is a hip-hop slang acronym that stands for *Pretty, Hot, and Tempting*. Basically, PHAT means attractive. You become attractive to be around. You ooze confidence. You create an aura of inevitability. You must believe you can help. That you *will* help. It is inevitable. At its core, having personal curb appeal is knowing that you can and will *be progress* for the people you meet.

Some times you are going to have to act more positive and confident than you feel. If you do, you will soon start to feel more positive and confident. Change the negative perceptions about yourself and you will easily build greater trust and rapport with others. I know this is almost impossible to pull off, but try to compete only with yourself and do not compare yourself with others. Your overriding goal is to be the best you can be.

Don't let anyone *(including yourself)* say you can't do it.

As a young student, Martin Luther King, Jr., was told by a teacher that he would never be able to speak with enough passion to motivate people into taking action.

Thomas Edison was told by educators that he was too stupid to comprehend anything.

Walt Disney was fired by a newspaper editor because he had "no good ideas."

Beethoven's music instructor once said of him, "As a composer, he is hopeless."

A magazine editor once informed Emily Dickinson that he could not publish her poems because they failed to rhyme.

Michael Jordan was cut from his high school basketball team at the start of his sophomore year.

Six Degrees of Practice

Networking is a skill. As with any skill, you will get better at it with practice. To have personal curb appeal, it is vital that you get over the stuff about networking that bothers you. If you are scared of meeting people or if you're worried about having nothing to say or becoming tongue-tied, role-play with a friend until you feel more confident.

The more you exercise your networking muscles, the stronger they get and the easier networking becomes. Networking is hard when you feel you HAVE to, and so easy when you feel you WANT to.

Attitudes are contagious.
Are yours worth catching?

Remember, networking is as natural as eating and sleeping. We do it all the time. Whenever you talk with others and ask their opinions to help you make an informed decision – even if it's just to find a good book, tire store, or dog groomer – you're networking. Networking is a vital quality-of-life skill that anyone can utilize to make more opportunities.

Meeting people is not really that tough, but connecting with people and making a great first impression is. With practice, great first impressions can be honed and perfected. Practice on strangers – even that dude wearing flip-flops in front of you in line at Mickey D's. Elevators are good places for a chat.

Start striking up conversations with strangers in lines *(grocery store checkout, movie ticket, hot dog stand, etc.)*. Make networking a habit. Practice every day, every chance you get.

Remember, every contact enlarges your net and gets you closer to the people who could enrich your life or utilize your products and services.

> **"You gotta try your luck at least once a day, because you could be going around lucky all day and not even know it."**
>
> *-- Jimmy Dean*

Speak to as many people as possible, get as many business cards as you can, and exchange e-mail addresses. Keep making contact. Keep in touch with those you wish to influence. Communicate regularly with pivotal people in your industry and in other industries. Many have enormous power that could help you gain access to almost anyone, many of whom you could never reach on your own.

If you have support from these people, you will save yourself a lot of time and trouble in getting where you want to go. Doors will seem to magically fly open for you.

You are only a few contacts away from a great opportunity.

Do you remember the **Six Degrees of Kevin Bacon** game? It was all the rage a few years back. The game is based on the main concept in John Guare's play *Six Degrees of Separation,* which was adapted into a movie with Will Smith. The play theorizes that we are all connected by six or fewer stages of circumstance or acquaintance.

Six Degrees of Kevin Bacon takes this concept one step further (or back). Kevin Bacon has been in a ton of movies and many of them were ensemble films, like *Diner* and *Mystic River.* If you use Kevin as an end point, you can link him in six steps (degrees) or fewer to almost any other performer.

For example, Kevin Bacon links to John Lithgow in one quick link:

Both were in *Footloose*. (1)

Kris Kristofferson, however, may take all six steps to make the chain. Let's see:

Kris was in *A Star Is Born* with Barbra Streisand. (1)
Barbra was in *The Way We Were* with Robert Redford. (2)
Robert was in *Brubaker* with Morgan Freeman. (3)
Morgan was in *Driving Miss Daisy* with Dan Ackroyd. (4)
Dan was in *The Blues Brothers* with John Belushi. (5)
John was in *Animal House* with Kevin Bacon. (6)

I'm sure you can get from Kris to Kevin in fewer moves, but I wanted to give an example of the full six degrees of separation.

Wildly Unimportant FYI:

I am linked to Kevin in two moves.
Dean was in Twister *with Bill Paxton. (1)*
Bill was in Apollo 13 *with Kevin Bacon. (2)*

Yes, I was in Twister. *Don't blink. The flying cow ended up with a bigger part than I did. I was one of the 'bad guys' driving the black vans.*

There is so much I could share that is interesting but not relevant to this topic.

I will share this: Bill Paxton is cool. Great everyman-type leader. Grade-A stuff. He makes everyone around him feel great. Bill Paxton rocks.

Conquering the
FEAR of Networking

One of the main reasons it is hard to have curb appeal when networking is FEAR.

What will people think when I walk across a room and approach them to start a conversation?
Will they think I am stupid, boring, pushy?
How's my breath?

It *can* be intimidating to approach someone and start a conversation. Ralph Waldo Emerson knew the way around this universal fear, but most of all he knew the way *through* it: *"Do the thing you fear and the death of fear is certain."*

Progress agents get all the butterflies in their stomach to fly in formation and then soar above their comfort zone to a new, more expansive comfort zone. Don't make networking more complicated than it needs to be. Develop strong networking skills so you can make connections without being rattled and intimidated. The more intimidated you are by the process, the less appealing you are in the process.

Emerson's advice will help you overcome the fear of meeting new people. Use Nike's formula and *Just Do It!* These new contacts may eventually become strategic partners, customers, employees, employers, or even best friends. Remember, most people enjoy offering assistance, information, and advice. No one is getting voted off the island at the end of the event.

"You are the one who can stretch your own horizon."
-- Rabbi Edgar F. Magnin

Zig Ziglar often uses a popular acronym for fear. He says fear stands for: **False Evidence Appearing Real.** *Right on, Zig.*

Really, do not be a Mumpsimus. No, that is not misspelled and no, I didn't call you a dirty word. Well, maybe I did – sort of.

Mumpsimus (*pronounced MUMP-si-mus*) is a seldom-used word. I was introduced to it by Rick Loy, the Vice President of Sales for AdvoCare (I highly recommend their SPARK drink).

Mumpsimus means:
A. a person who persists in a mistaken expression or practice.
B. an erroneous practice, use of language, or belief that is
*   obstinately adhered to.*

In other words, the unfortunate state of mumpsimus means pigheaded adherence to a notion or expression that is popular but obviously wrong. Do not be a mumpsimus about networking. It is not some bad, hard, or artificial experience. Resist the popular notion that networking is all fake sincerity and pushy behavior. That is just not so.

Networking is not about arm-twisting. It is not trying to get someone to do something that does not make sense for them to do. It is not scary old backslapping sales shenanigans. The simple fact is, most people are cool and want to meet you. You will not find Eeyore or Oscar the Grouch at most networking events.

I do need to mention, though, that no matter how cool, giving, and funny you are, there are going to be some folks who just don't get it. They are not interested in anything or anybody, and are always bummed out.

My quick advice is: *Move on.* Do not let their flawed human thing rock you. Really, who can honestly say they enjoy talking to a negative blowhard? People like this expect the worst and that is exactly what they get. Somebody forgot to tell them that you create your own reality and if you expect bad stuff to happen, bad stuff happens.

You know the people I am talking about – the ones who look and act like they just ate a big steaming bowl of "Catcher in the Rye." They're irritable, easily agitated, restless types who love a good argument. Chances are, they are not *feeling* too wonderful, either. They have no personal curb appeal.

So what are the possible causes of soreheaditus?

Maybe their back is out of alignment. That could make you a sourpuss.
Financial and personal problems can make someone a bellyacher.
Hating your job can make you crabby.
A bad haircut can undercut confidence.
Alan Greenspan's latest is not the greatest.
A hangnail.
Hunger.
Perhaps it's Monday.

Come to think of it, a lot of things can make people habitually irritable.

So how come more people are not walking around scowling and biting the heads off of bats? (Maybe because bats are hard to catch?). I'll tell you the real reason. It's all in their attitude. Those disgruntled people CHOOSE their bummed reaction to the world because they do not know how else to deal with it.

They need a little Monty Python. They need to *"Always Look on the Bright Side of Life."* Progress agents have discovered that changing the way they look at things makes life easier in all aspects.

Think of Oscar the Grouch types as just nice people who have not yet been taught how to cope with life's stresses and challenging moments. Taking responsibility for themselves and their choices has never occurred to them before. Maybe they grew up in a dysfunctional family and had no suitable role models to show them more appropriate ways of responding.

Progress agents always set a good example for faultfinders to follow. We adopt the "live and help prosper" philosophy, and we are not quick to make judgments.

So you can choose to tactfully walk away from a new contact who is letting off negative steam, or you can choose to stay a little while, lend a sympathetic ear, and try to guide the person to a new way of thinking. Friendly words of wisdom shared at the *appropriate* moment *might* make a difference. But be careful because uninvited advice is sometimes seen as a form of attack.

Do not take responsibility for these people or take their Holden Caulfield impression personally (Holden is the hilariously agitated protagonist and narrator of the JD Salinger novel, *The Catcher in the Rye)*. They are probably bummed at the whole wide world. They may have been like this for most of their lives and they are probably not going to change just because you chatted with them for five to eight minutes at a business mixer.

But most people are cool, nice, enjoyable, and are there to connect. If they are not, they are making a far worse impression than you are.

Shrug it off. Do not let these sad sacks curb your enthusiasm.

Have fun.
Enjoy the process.

Life is too short *(for you and everyone else)*.

Mumpsimus Revisited:

The generally accepted story of the word's origin is found in the 1517 writing of Richard Pace, a humanist and friend of Sir Thomas More. Pace later became the Dean of St Paul's Cathedral in London.

Pace tells of a medieval monk who persisted in saying "quod in ore mumpsimus" instead of "quod in ore sumpsimus" when celebrating mass. "Sumpsimus" is Latin for "we have taken," and the full phrase translates to "which we have taken into the mouth." "Mumpsimus" is just babble.

It isn't clear whether the well-seasoned monk was illiterate (though that is the general assumption) or whether the word was transcribed incorrectly in his copy of the mass. What made this particular mistake memorable is that when a younger monk tried to correct the old guy, the older man replied that he had been saying it that way for over forty years and added, "I will not change my old mumpsimus for your new sumpsimus."

And that is how 'mumpsimus' came to mean:
A. a person who persists in a mistaken expression or practice.
B. an erroneous practice, use of language, or belief that is obstinately adhered to.

Not sure if you wanted to know, but now you do.

Your Mind Is a Terrible Thing to Use Against Yourself

Remember, you have good stuff to share. Like yourself – but never be cocky or vain. Like who you are on the *inside*. If you don't like yourself – *Big Problem*. Far too many people go around disliking themselves, focusing in on the negatives. This is a huge part of the reason why substance abuse, gambling, depression, anxiety, stress-related physical disorders, obesity, and other eating disorders are all galloping epidemics. Negative self-thoughts aren't just self-limiting, they can kill you.

Find a way to feel good about yourself. Hang with people who – like PBS's Mister Rogers – *"like you just the way you are."* Allow their views to rub off on you. Make yourself appealing to yourself. *Say it with me: I'm OK. You're OK.*

We each have a wealth of ideas, experiences, contacts, and resources that others need. Recognize and use these strengths of yours. Develop a healthy self-concept. I do not want to go all Dr. Phil on you, but you have to go inside before you can go outside.

We need to be real careful about what we say to ourselves and believe about ourselves. Henry Ford is quoted as saying "Whether you think you can or think you can't – you're right." Around the same time, Luigi Pirandello wrote a play that said the same thing: *Right You Are, If You Think You Are.*

Yes, I am talking about *affirmations*. When I realized that I was going to passionately encourage people to focus on affirmations, I admit I had nightmares of Stuart Smalley (Al Franken's character from "Saturday Night Live"): *"I'm good enough, I'm smart enough, and doggone it, people like me."*

Affirmations just seemed so wishy-washy, so flimsy. But I dug deeper and came to realize that we use affirmations all the time. It's just that most of them are negative and self-limiting:

"I have a short attention span."
"I am not good at meeting people."
"I participate in road rage."

Our brains are trippy and complicated and can do amazing things. But at their core our brains want one thing – ***To Be Right.***

Whatever we continually say about ourselves and start to believe about ourselves, our brains are going to work to make it true. It is imperative that we be careful about the things we say to ourselves because…

"Whatever you say to yourself, you're right."

Try using self-empowering affirmations and visualizations to create a more positive attitude about yourself.

Stuff like:

"I believe in myself."
"I am always interested in meeting new people."
"Every day I make good decisions that positively affect my life."
"This is a really good book."

Enjoy yourself. Mingle and keep it light.

Go to networking events *expecting* to have a positive experience. As with any sales strategy:

If you think networking is a bad idea,
you will prove yourself RIGHT.

Always act like an equal – because you are. Sure, some in the room make more money than you today, but real wealth is measured by what you are and not by how much you have. I know that sounds hokey, but it is still true.

You can act your way to better feelings, but rarely can you feel your way to better actions. Repetition is the mother of skill and competence. Feelings follow actions and behavior. Do not wait to network when you feel like it, or you may never get rolling.

Far too many professionals never network enough to develop the confidence that comes with experience. They do not go through the networking process enough to get comfortable.

Don't feel that you're good at conversation?
Ask great questions and listen *(a list of good questions is found on pages 97-98)*.

Also, start reading for thirty minutes a day. Take in all the information you can. Read anything and everything so you can carry your share of the conversation.

Live in a hockey town?
Read the hockey scores even if you don't know the meaning of a hat trick *(Google it)*. Pull your conversational weight.

Be a student of the universe. Register and regularly attend classes at Universe University. Universe U. UU. U squared. Knowledge about many issues and trends makes you more interesting. People coming in contact with you will more likely want to associate with you if you are well-read and knowledgeable *(as long as what you are well-read and knowledgeable about isn't just* TV Guide *and the* National Enquirer*)*.

Suggested reading:

Your local newspapers
Your local business journal
Your industry trade journals and newsletter
Publications that relate to your personal interests and specific industry.

Magazines:

    Fast Company, Time, Newsweek, Selling Power, Fortune

Books:

    Man's Search for Meaning – Viktor Frankl
    Let's Get Real or Let's Not Play – Mahan Khalsa
    Guerrilla Marketing – Jay Conrad Levinson
    The Secret – Ken Blanchard and Mark Miller
    Getting Rich Your Own Way – Brian Tracy
    It's Your Ship – Captain D. Michael Abrashoff
    The New Science of Selling and Persuasion – Bill Brooks
    Permission Marketing – Seth Godin
    The Ant and the Elephant – Vince Poscente
    Your Signature Work – Dianna Booher
    How to Win Friends and Influence People – Dale Carnegie
    Charisma – Dr. Tony Alessandra
    Relationship Selling – Jim Cathcart
    The 22 Immutable Laws of Marketing –
                Al Ries and Jack Trout
    The Millionaire Next Door –
                Thomas Stanley and William Danko
    And anything by:
    Tom Peters, Peter Drucker or GOD *(I like the Bible).*

Don't have time to read?
Try listening to books on tape in your car.

Bring the whole package to the party. How you look and what you wear matters, too. Perception counts. How you feel you look also has a big impact on how confident you will feel at the event. People can pick up on how you feel about yourself, and whether you feel you have personal curb appeal. Dress and groom with care, knowing that what you wear conveys a message to others as well as to yourself.

Get enough sleep, eat healthy food *(whatever that is this week – I hear some veggies may still be good for you),* exercise, and watch your weight. I am not saying this stuff just because it will make you look better to the people you meet *(although that never hurts).* I am encouraging you to take care of yourself and eat right for two major reasons:

A. You need to be proud of yourself and how you look.
B. You need energy *(and not the quick sugar rush of a honey-glazed donut).*

"Food is an important part of a balanced diet."
-- Fran Lebowitz

Be a success in your own eyes. Have an aura of progress. Create Personal Curb Appeal.

OK Corralled

The expression OK started as kind of a joke. During the late 1830s, in newspapers around Boston, it was considered super funny to shorten a phrase to initials only and then supply an explanation in parentheses. Sometimes the abbreviations were misspelled to add to the humor. OK was used as an abbreviation for "all correct," the joke being that neither the O nor the K was correct.

I'm All Correct. You're All Correct.

Step 2

O - Open Face-to-Face Relationships

Get Out and About

The second step in *Cracking the Networking CODE*
is to proactively:

Open Face-to-Face Relationships.

The key is to create and stick to a networking strategy. Proactively seek new contacts. Develop your plan of action and get started without delay. Identify who you want to meet, where you are likely to meet them, and how you will follow up. Invest quality time thinking about the people who can best offer you the right information, contacts, and opportunities. Build relationships with these people by understanding what you have to offer them.

Where are the best places to make face-to-face contact with them? Answering this question will help you decide which organizations you should belong to and which events you should attend. Important point: The organizations that are the best fit will change over time as your business grows and your career develops.

Go with realistic expectations. You are (probably) not going to land a big account or forge an automatic *strong* link from a five-minute encounter. Networking takes patience! Networking takes persistence! Come to terms with the fact that it is probably going to take more than one meeting for folks to come to the conclusion that you are amazingly with-it and that you offer progress for their lives.

In fact, it has been proven that it takes most people **six to eight positive impressions** to remember and begin to trust a new person. Keep firmly in your mind that networking may not provide immediate benefits. It may take years to see the results of your

61

networking efforts, or you could open your e-mail in the morning and have a cool opportunity from someone you connected with the day before.

Shy? Nervous? *That's understandable.*
Start with people you know and trust. Share your desire to be introduced to quality individuals who would be good for you to know. Get connected to the people your contacts know.

Vary your activities.
Grow your list of contacts each week. Start now and do not stop. If you're planning to hit several networking events in a single day, make sure you take time out to recharge. Plan your schedule so that you have periods of solitude. Guard against scheduling a full day of networking activities if you plan to network at an evening event. You're after quality, not quantity.

As you and your network grow, you will need to make some changes. Let go of organizations and associations you can no longer manage properly, or that are no longer compatible. Allow your network to evolve with you.

Have a goal for each event.
Decide what you hope to gain before you go. Write it down. Then get there and work toward it. Commit to staying until you have met and connected with your predetermined number or selection of people. Think about it. Set a target and push yourself. This will keep you from walking aimlessly around the room.

Keep a log.
For a month, keep a log of everyone you meet.
Then classify and analyze them.
Which contacts are most valuable? Where did you meet them?
Who are the takers and who are the givers?
Any time-wasters? Hey, your time is valuable too.

37 Questions for Defining
a Powerful Networking Plan

Before you get too far along in networking, ask yourself these 37 questions. Your answers will guide you in making wise investments of your time, and help you build the most constructive relationships.

1. *Why do you want a larger and/or better network of contacts?*

2. *What are the characteristics of a high-quality contact?*

3. *Are you looking for more business?*

4. *What type of business?*

5. *More of the same kinds of opportunities, or different opportunities?*

Identify the gaps in your network. Maybe your network is limited to only knowing people in your particular industry. It is a big, continually growing, diverse business world out there and your network needs to reflect that.

6. *Do you know too many people with similar backgrounds, or who think the same way?*

7. *With whom do you need to build a relationship?*

8. *Who can help you build your business or develop your career?*

9. *Who are the people whose opinions are most valued in your industry?*

10. *How can each person you identify contribute to your success?*

11. *What can you do for these people so they will want to be in a relationship with you?*

12. *What do you have to offer them? What's in it for them?*

13. *Where will you find these people?*

14. *How will you arrange to meet them?*

15. *Who can offer an introduction to the people you wish to meet?*

16. *What will you say to them that will elicit their interest in you?*

17. *Why would anyone want to remember you?*

18. *How can you nurture the relationship?*

19. *How can you earn a place in their lives?*

20. *How likable are you?*

21. *How trustworthy?*

22. *Do you make a point of speaking well of others?*

23. *Are people right in thinking of you as an expert?*

24. *What are your priorities and objectives for a particular event?*

25. *Why do customers choose you or your business over your competitors?*

26. *How can you prove to others that they can rely on your word?*

27. *Are you known as someone who under-promises and over-delivers, or as one who over-promises and delivers squat?*

28. *What is the buzz or word-of-mouth about you?*

29. *What is the buzz about your company?*

30. *What is the buzz about your service?*

31. *When you accept an invitation to an event or party, do the hosts have doubts that you will actually show up?*

32. *Do you show up?*

33. *How many people would stake their reputation on you?*

34. *What are people saying about your work ethic?*

35. *Who initiates most of your business or social conversations?*

Look, if others are not striking up conversations with you or inviting you out, this might be saying something about you and how you are perceived.

Finally, always ask yourself these two basic questions when going to any networking event. Remember to focus on finding the answers while at the function.

36. *How can I make events I attend more beneficial for others?*

37. *How can I benefit each person I meet?*

Sometimes it may appear one-sided, but in the world of networking - **What Goes Around, Comes Around.**

16 Examples of Proven Places to Network

You can and should open relationships everywhere. On Planes, Trains, and Automobiles. On Golden Pond and even on the Bridge on the River Kwai. *(Sorry, I got carried away and my movie references got a tad silly.)* Anyway, you get the point.

To make connecting easier and more focused, look for groups and events where networking is encouraged. People expect to exchange cards and meet new people at these types of gatherings, so go expecting to make some contacts.

It is best not to consider joining any business organizations unless you are committed to being an *active member* for at least one year. This stuff takes time.

Too many people go to business networking events with the wrong focus and try to force their service down your throat. If you are not on the top of your game, you will end up stoically listening to a bunch of pitches instead of getting the person to have a real conversation.

Also, it is possible to spend a bunch of dinero on joining networking groups, so consider your affiliations carefully. Call and ask if you can attend as a visitor. Most allow at least one free visit.

Again, you SHOULD network everywhere and anywhere. Start your own networking group. There are plenty of places that offer networking possibilities. What follows is by no means a complete list, but these suggestions can lead to other opportunities.

16 Examples of Proven Places to Network:

1. Organizations to Which You Already Belong

The first place to start networking is in the organizations you already belong to. Anywhere you are already connected: your homeowners' association, office parties, Sunday school class, PTA, workout club, sports groups, political party meetings, Junior League. Anywhere.

2. Professional and Trade Associations

Your professional trade association can put you in touch with colleagues in your field. Cultivate relationships with other members, tap into their expertise, discuss industry concerns, and swap ideas. These are usually the best organizations for gaining fresh insight into your industry, your clients, and *your competition.*

Check out your membership directory to find experts in the profession. Contact them for advice or ideas. The sooner you get involved in your trade association, the sooner your name will get out there. Serve on committees, contribute articles to the group's publications, speak at conferences, run for the board. Learn and practice new skills at educational seminars. You can learn how to use emerging technologies and catch up on new techniques. Read the association's newsletter for tips on how to succeed and use the full benefits of membership. Contact supplier members. They can tell you about new products and services used in your industry.

3. State and National Trade Shows, Conventions, and Conferences

Business and industry trade shows, conventions, and conferences have great potential as really solid places to network. However, a bewildering number of people never take advantage of these solid opportunities even when they go, because they treat the trip as a much deserved paid vacation instead of one of the best spots in the cosmos to make new contacts. This is not the place to let your hair down and get your groove on.

Some of the big trade shows draw participants from around the globe. So much potential! At breakfast, lunch, dinner, and networking activities, meet as many people as possible, get their cards and stay in touch. Study the schedule and ask the organizers for a list of attendees before you go. Formulate a plan to make it a valuable investment of time and money. *(See pages 73-76 for tips on running a successful trade show booth.)*

At conventions, try contacting keynoters and concurrent-session presenters ahead of time. *Most often we speakers are from out of town and do not know anyone, so invite us to sit with you during lunch, or schedule time for a cup of coffee.* At least introduce yourself to the presenters and those sitting around you.

4. Trade Organizations of Your Best Customers
If the fine people who already use your services belong to these organizations, would it not be safe to assume that other members might want to use your services as well? See if you can present a breakout session or seminar on something related to your work.

5. Chamber of Commerce
They don't call them Chambers of Commerce for nothing. More than likely, your community's Chamber of Commerce is in the position to serve as your greatest local establishment for making priceless business relationships, but only if you're active and informed. Most Chambers welcome guests at functions but are usually only interested in recommending their members. The upside is that you can join as a business or as an individual.

Chambers sponsor networking activities like after-hours mixers, business-networking breakfasts, luncheons, and even leads groups. Chamber events are great forums for sharpening your skills and opening face-to-face relationships.

6. Organizations with the Same Philosophy as Yours

If you care about the purpose of the organization, you will be proud to be a member and reap personal satisfaction, along with the opportunity to build relationships. Get involved in a charity that feels right.

7. Small Business Development Centers - SBDC

Most metropolitan areas have a couple of SBDCs. Whether you have your own business or are an employee, these business centers offer courses and resources to help you to grow, as well as to meet people.

8. Hobby/Passion

Join groups that offer possibilities for making contacts and achieving personal growth: art appreciation, dancing, chess, astronomy, wine and food clubs, etc. You will meet others with similar interests who are ready to network. Go to meetings that feature discussions on a topic you're interested in.

9. Golf/ Sports

Golf has long been *the* sport for business networking. So if you're a somewhat decent swinger, tee up. Jerry Lindsay (successful business owner, avid golfer, and a great dad) offers these words of caution: *"The way a person relates to golf mirrors the way they relate to business. So putt everything out, play the ball where it lies, let faster players play through, do not throw clubs, and most of all, do not cheat."* Other sports work fine for networking, too. The key is to find a sport you are interested in, and get involved.

10. Spiritual Organizations

I am NOT suggesting that you join a church or synagogue only for the business opportunities. But let's face it – many solid business relationships are forged in the pews and folding chairs of spiritual organizations. Go for the right reasons and let your light shine. *Hide it under a bushel?* No. You've got to let it shine.

11. Workshops, Classes, and Seminars
Take every chance to learn more and make yourself better. Other
people committed to jogging the road to success will be there too.
Contribute ideas. Ask questions. Look for a list of upcoming
workshops in your local business journal's calendar of events.
Expect a higher grade of professionals at the workshops and
seminars that are sponsored by area business journals.

12. College Associations
Having common backgrounds makes for easy conversations and
many really get a kick out of helping an alum of their university.

13. Leads Groups
The great thing about leads groups is that they are focused on lead
generation for their members. Expect events held by leads groups to
be more intense than the rest of the networking options on this list.

Make sure you check out the membership roster before you join. If
there are some members who are in your line of work, you will
probably want to join another leads group. They may not even let
you join if there is already someone in your category. Also, find out
what the member obligations are, and ask some of the members how
much business they have generated from being a member.

14. Kiwanis, Rotary, AMBUCS, Lions, Elks, Moose
(I know there is an animal joke in there somewhere.) Do good for
the community while you build relationships. Rock-solid plan.
Here it really pays to serve as a leader.

15. Cultural Events
Meet some people with style and taste. Theater, symphony, art
exhibits, rodeos, tractor pulls ...

16. Volunteer

A great way to gain visibility and develop relationships is through volunteering with any of the above-listed groups. Almost all these groups could use a hand. Step out and step up. Look for volunteer jobs that will provide you opportunities to show off your skills and personality, and meet and interact with new contacts. You increase your impact as well as the potential for new contacts when you actively participate.

Volunteer to:

- Serve on committees. You can help shape the association's policy, as well as work closely with and learn from other experts.

- Chair a committee or run for office. Let people experience your leadership, communication, and organizational skills in action.

- Work the reception desk. You will meet people as they sign in.

- Help direct people to the right rooms at a large convention (often called being a *people mover*).

- Be a greeter. The greeter spot is ideal for the self-diagnosed shy, because the title alone forces you to connect. Plus, as a greeter there is an automatic assumption that you are "in the know" and others will naturally come to you for info and help.

- Join the board. You will connect with key industry leaders and gain a reputation as a leader yourself.

16 Tips for Running a Successful Trade Show Booth

Working a booth at a trade show can be such a powerful way to network, reinforce existing relationships, and build name recognition that I wanted to offer some insight into making the most of the investment. The key is to find ways to encourage visitors to stop and comfortably begin building a relationship with you. Here are sixteen surefire ways to build priceless business relationships running a trade show booth.

1. Build rapport by being friendly and nonthreatening.
A smile goes a long way in welcoming people to visit your booth.

> **"Every business is built on friendship."**
> *-- James Cash Penney*

2. Create the right first impression.
Stand and be interested in making contact. Do not sit, read, drink, eat, or smoke in the booth. Don't just chat away with the people working the booth with you. This makes you less approachable.

3. Keep the booth looking sharp.
Do not let the booth get disorganized, cluttered, or untidy. Throw trash away. If skirted, the space under the table is a great place to store boxes and stuff. Many trade shows last weeks. Even if it is a lengthy show, do not let your booth get run down.

4. Avoid drinking alcohol or eating spicy or garlicky foods.
Bad breath is bad business – as is slurred speech and inappropriate behavior. *You do not want to be remembered as the drunk guy, or halitosis girl.*

73

5. Ask open-ended questions.

Avoid asking questions that can be answered with a yes or no. Create a list of questions to ask that begin with who, what, where, when, why, or how. This will stimulate thought and encourage conversation. Relate questions to the event, industry, product/service and its benefits, or to a specific situation.

Examples of Stimulating Questions:

What brought you out to the show today?
How could you see using this (product/service)?
How important is (benefit) in your present situation?
What are your most important needs in (situation)?
How familiar are you with our product/company/service?

Steer clear of common and overused questions, like:

How are you doing today?
Can I help you?
Are you enjoying the show?

6. Wear your corporate logo.

This shows professionalism and teamwork and makes you easily identifiable with the booth. Also, when you walk around the show, you are getting a little extra exposure. Don't have quality shirts with your logo on them? Get them. No time? Wear your professionally made company nametags. Do the trade show, then get some shirts.

7. Wear comfortable shoes.

You should be on your feet all day so do not wear new shoes or high heels. Come 3:45 P.M., you will be glad you took this advice.

8. Do not leave the booth unattended.
This means you will need to have a team. Trade off so you can take breaks and roam the show.

9. Make the most of every meal.
Prearrange breakfast, lunch, and dinner meetings with key people at the show.

10. Do not complain about being at the show, use inappropriate language or off-color humor. You'd be stunned at how often I hear people dissing the show, swearing, or cracking a risqué joke. Bad form. Bad business, or should I say, no business!

11. Do not badmouth your competitors.
Badmouthing competitors makes you appear less confident about your products/services and especially about yourself. It also shines an unnecessary spotlight on the competitor. Bring up the good points about your stuff and leave badmouthing the competitors to your ecstatic customers.

12. Do not eat at your booth.
I'm sure you would agree that it's not attractive to watch someone chow down on nachos smothered in that bright orange fake cheese gunk. What is worse is when they see you coming and they lick their fingers while looking around for a napkin to wipe off the grease so they can reach out to shake your hand. The need for nourishment is another solid reason to find someone you can trust to run your booth while you go get a bite to eat.

13. Get a list of attendees and contact them before the show.
Send them an invitation to your booth. Make them want to visit your booth. Offer a giveaway, or announce that you are unveiling something new to the market they must know about. Look over the list of attendees for heavy hitters and personally ask them to visit your booth.

14. Get business cards/contact information.

This is HUGE. How else are you going to follow up? Offer your company's free e-mail newsletter. Don't have one? Start one. Have a giveaway, a drawing, or some kind of contest. Ask for cards. You have to be able to reconnect and market to these people after the event.

15. Take notes.

So many people, so little brain space! Write a few words on the back of cards that will help you remember the person, the conversation, or the opportunity. This will go a long way toward making # 16 happen.

16. Follow up in a timely manner.

This is where it so often falls apart. You **MUST** reconnect with the folks you met. Thank them for visiting your booth. Mention something interesting they shared with you. Look at your NOTES. Do not do this three weeks after the show. Do it the next day. Don't try to hard-sell them in the follow-up, just make a pleasurable second impression and see if there are ways you can serve this person, even if it is not with your stuff.

Trade shows are powerful and profitable places to grow your network if you are prepared and know how to work them.

Nine Proven Strategies for Opening Face-to-Face Relationships

Here are nine proven strategies for making contact at networking events.

1. Know as much as you can about the attendees.
Research the people you want to meet. Before the event, ask the sponsors of the event for a list of attendees and create your most-wanted "hit list" of people you definitely want to connect with. When calling organizers to RSVP for an event, ask for information about people in your focus market or VIPs who might be attending. That way, you will have two or three people in mind who you would like to meet when you arrive.

2. Go it alone.
When attending networking functions, go by yourself or at least communicate to your carpool buddies that you should all fan out. Moving about a networking event solo encourages people to approach you and makes it easy to mingle and initiate conversations. It may be more comfortable to have a friend right there with you, but remember: you are there to grow your network, not hang with the people already in your network.

3. Stand near the registration table.
After you have registered and put on your nametag, take advantage of the many opportunities to make small talk with new arrivals after they have signed in. These are the couple of minutes when most people are alone and interested in someone new to communicate with. Even something really easygoing like, "Looks like a good turnout..." is probably good enough to get a friendly conversation started. Remember that like you, people are there to make new contacts. And if they are not, they are in the wrong place.

77

4. Get an introduction to the person you want to meet.
An introduction is an implied endorsement. Try to get introduced
by the most respected person at the event with whom you have a
relationship. Solid CODE crackers are always happy to play a part
in your success and you look like a winner by association.

Who are the people who have established a good reputation?
Who loves to network and knows a lot of people?

These people have a large circle of influence and understand the
power of networking. They are quick to bond and make the most of
relationships. *(Be sure to ask them if there is someone you can
introduce them to.)*

Who are the solid networkers inside your network?

Find out what they do. Study the techniques of a successful
networker. Try to tag along with a well-connected person in your
network to some of their normal networking functions and ask them
to introduce you to a few of their contacts. Give them some insight
and direction by letting them know the kind of person you want to
meet – the more specific the better.

A slight modification on the same strategy
Look for someone you know who is chatting with a couple of people
you do not know. Approach the group and stand to the side within
view of the person you know. This serves as a subtle cue for your
contact to introduce you to the group and bring you into the
conversation. *Try it. It works.* If someone invites you to join the
group but forgets to introduce you, take the initiative and introduce
yourself.

> **"When the character of a man is not clear
> to you, look at his friends."**
> *-- Japanese Proverb*

5. Study the tags.
If nametags are preprinted and on display at the registration table, scan the tags of the other attendees to see what opportunities await you.

Though I have not tried this myself, Rachel Wood, a top financial advisor in the Boston area who introduced herself to me after one of my seminars on networking, does something pretty neato. If she spots a nametag on the registration table of someone she would like to meet, she asks the people manning the table if she can clip a note to their tag saying she would like to meet them. She swears by it.

By the way:
Leave your ego there at the registration desk. The first positive impression is the most important, and lays the groundwork for all future impressions. You want to make sure you are making a good one.

6. Circle and scan.
Before diving into the event, try circling the room and checking out the nametags for people or companies you definitely want to make contact with while there.

7. Look for people standing alone.
These folks may be nervous, and your initiative will often endear you to them. Plus, one-on-one networking is the best networking. It is hard to join a group unless invited.

8. Sit between people you do not know well.
If the event is a sit-down affair, **do not sit by a friend or business associate.** You already know that person! You might be sitting there a while, so make sure you are going to be sitting by someone you can form a *new* relationship with. Plan who you want to sit by, but wait until the last minute to actually sit down so you can keep making new contacts.

9. Hang out at the food table.
I know it sounds like I'm joking, but people tend to be easily
accessible around food. Stand near the food table, but not the bar.
People tend to grab their drinks and move away from the bar,
but are more likely to linger near the grub.

As people check out the buffet table, small talk comes more easily.
"That Danish looks good..." is as good an opener as any. Once they
have their hands full, people often look for a flat surface where they
can place their plate and beverage. Take a spot next to them and get
to chatting.

Check this out.
Our endorphin levels are higher when we are close to food, which
boosts our memory and the chance that we will remember and be
remembered. *We humans are a trip, aren't we?*

> **"If more of us valued food and cheer and song
> above hoarded gold, it would be a merrier world."**
> *-- JRR Tolkien*

Do not go to networking functions hungry.
Eat before you go so you can focus on the person, not the
cantaloupe. If you are hungry, grab a quick bite off to the side, and
then mingle. Do not talk with your mouth full. *(I hope I didn't need
to write that.)*

Six Often Overlooked
Networking Opportunities

Here are six often overlooked opportunities for opening face-to-face relationships.

1. Speak at conferences.
Speaking in public strikes big fear in the hearts and minds of the unprepared. It is the #1 fear for a lot of people, one slot above death. But speaking has the power to position you as an expert, a leader, a thinker in your community and your industry.

Join Toastmasters (www.toastmasters.org) to get over the fear and polish the tools needed to become a confident speaker and a successful networker. Toastmasters can help you become an interesting person and a valuable resource to others by sharpening your communications skills. You'll gain self-confidence and learn to present a great first impression. Get ready, because with Toastmasters there are live speaking opportunities from the get-go.

2. Follow your money.
Who are your suppliers?
Where do you spend money?
What places do you frequent?

Get to know your vendors better. If you are their customer, they probably serve other topnotch business professionals like you, right? Find out who else they know. Their contacts could be worth more than the service or products they provide. Work to build the exchange of contacts into the relationships. Ask them to recommend you. A nifty by-product of relationship-building is you will likely improve the quality of your service.

3. Help others become better networkers.

Offer proven strategies and techniques for effective self-marketing and relationship-building. As your contacts' networks grow and strengthen, so do yours.

> **"The greatest good we can do for others is not to share our riches, but to assist in revealing their own."**
> *-- Benjamin Disraeli*

4. Hug a "gatekeeper."

Make friends with the executive assistants of those you want to create a relationship with. Executive assistants can become solid allies or your worst nightmare. Do not make the mistake of taking them for granted or seeing them as obstacles to be overcome.

Heck, they're the ones who set up appointments for the decision maker. And in a lot of cases…

THEY *ARE* THE DECISION MAKERS.

Get to know everyone in the office as individuals. Talk with them. Learn all the front-office folks' names, special interests and hobbies, the names of their kids, and stuff like that. Check for clues from what they display on their desks.

Be dependable and genuine. If you can build a solid bond with these key individuals, you will differentiate yourself from run-of-the-mill sales punks who ignore gatekeepers and just try to barge in to see the big chief.

If gatekeepers know and respect you, they can recommend you when the need for your service arises. They can keep you in the loop. They can be your greatest champion. Plus, executives respect you more if you have an authentic interest in their whole staff. Most executives like and respect their assistants and value their insight, so if the assistant likes you, so will the person in charge.

To gain a possible inside track, ask assistants what groups their boss is active in. Join those groups and get involved. When decision makers see you engaged in activities outside of the office, they develop more confidence and respect for you. *That's good.*

5. Include your friends and neighbors.

Far too often, we already know people with the right contacts or expertise, but we do not know it. It is imperative to get to know everyone in your existing network on a more solid footing.

Find out who your closest friends and colleagues know. It is probably worthwhile for you to get to know more of your friends' friends and your neighbors' neighbors (of course, you are first going to have to actually meet your neighbors). You never know where your next opportunity, job, or client will come from, so do not rule out your friends and relatives as possible contacts. Your Uncle Abbott may have a neighbor who has a son who needs exactly what your company has to offer.

6. Bond with the spouses and significant others of the influential.

The influence and power wielded by spouses and significant others is grossly underestimated. And because of this, they often go ignored. When offered the chance at a function, invest the time to make a solid connection with them. Get to know them as people, and after the event they are likely to speak well of you to the very person you targeted.

Step 3

D - Deliver Solid First Impressions

20 Quick Tips for Delivering
Solid First Impressions

The third step in *Cracking the Networking CODE* is to:
Deliver Solid First Impressions.

Building a relationship entails a series of impressions. None is more important than the first. Make sure your first meeting with someone is powerful. Remember, people meet people all the time. You need to stand out as someone they want future contact with. *Here are 20 quick tips for delivering solid first impressions.*

1. Do not try to do major business deals (save that for later).
Do not rush new relationships; think LONG TERM. Do not SELL! It is a mind-set. Be subtle. The worst thing you could do is try to start selling someone as soon as you meet them.

2. Get revved up.
If you want people to have a positive feeling toward you, first create this emotion within yourself. Everyone is, at some level, nervous about meeting new people. It is common to tense up when you are about to walk into a networking group. Do whatever it takes to get yourself revved up and at the same time calm your nerves before the event. Try these to help get you straight *(somewhere you won't look stupid):*
– *Roll your shoulders. Clap your hands. Stretch. Shake it out!*
– *Stretch out your jaw (to avoid clenching your teeth).*
– *Do breathing exercises: Breathe in for the count of five and breathe out for the count of ten. Do this five or six more times.*
– *Listen to motivational tapes or your favorite music – loud – in your car. If you feel like it, sing along.*

3. Catch that name.

We say we *forget* names. But I don't think that's true. I don't think we really *hear* the name of the person when we meet them. We are not listening. We are more focused on what we're about to say. The other person's name is way important to them, probably about as important as yours is to you. To make a great first impression, make a point of *catching* and *tossing around* the person's name in conversation. This is almost impossible when we are preoccupied with what we are going to do or say next to be impressive.

> ### *The Name Game*
> 1. Right before you meet new people,
>   PREPARE to CATCH their name.
> 2. Toss their name back in your first or second response.
> 3. Mention their name naturally throughout the conversation (but do not overdo it).
> 4. Repeat their name when parting.

If you do not catch it, ask them to repeat it rather than letting it go. Do not be embarrassed to ask *(they probably did not catch your name either)*. Read others' nametags. That's what they're there for.

Again, your new contact's name is the ultimate word to use in order to make a solid first impression. Using the person's name in a natural manner throughout the conversation is an easy and organic way to create a memorable link between yourself and your new contact.

4. Be an Early Bird and a Late Bloomer.

Never be late. At a networking event the ten minutes before things get under way and the ten minutes after are the real golden moments. So arrive 15 minutes early and stay 15 minutes late.

5. Always stand when meeting someone new.

It shows respect. *What else can I say about it?*

6. Hand in hand.

In the business arena, handshakes are the accepted greeting. As a rule, I would advise against initiating kisses or hugs in a business setting. Take the handshake seriously; you *will* be judged by the quality (limp/firm, moist/dry, lengthy/brief) of your handshake. Above all, a handshake should be firm, *but not bone-crushing*. No dead fish handshakes. They're creepy.

Note to men about shaking hands with women:
Don't wimp out on the handshake. I often hear from female professionals I am working with how some men will offer them a lame *"I don't want to hurt you – you delicate flower, you"* handshake. Be a man. Shake the hand.

You can avoid delivering a cold, wet handshake by keeping your drink in the left hand. If your hands tend to be clammy, try spraying them with antiperspirant at least once a day. Also, try carrying Kleenex in your pocket and drying your hands discreetly from time to time. To really put yourself over the top, shake hands good-bye as well as hello.

7. Look them in the eyes.

You do not want to stare at them but you do need to look people in the eyes if you want them to start trusting you. If you find it difficult to offer or establish direct eye contact, challenge yourself to know what color the person's eyes are by the time you have asked your second question.

8. Travel light.

In most cases, there is no need to take your briefcase or even a purse. You do not want to have to put down all that stuff (brochures, briefcases, or handbags) and dig out a business card. It's also tougher to move around or look comfortable and easygoing with your arms filled with your company's propaganda. Remember, you are there to connect, not sell.

9. Meet. Talk. Get card. Go.

At a networking event, talk to one person for about four to five minutes – eight minutes maximum. Get their card, take some notes, and work toward a comfortable conclusion to this initial conversation. Hogging someone's time is an inexcusable no-no. If you cannot find a natural way to end the conversation, introduce the person to someone else. It's a win-win. You help them connect with someone new and you get to move on without appearing rude.

10. Do not act desperate for business.

People want to talk to upbeat, confident people. You will not create any priceless business relationships if you act like you don't have lunch money. Treat people as worthy of your respect and courtesy, not as targets.

11. Wear your nametag *(on your right side).*

Always wear a nametag at networking functions. This makes you easily accessible. Think of it as a sticky advertisement. The reason you wear it on the right is that when you shake hands with your right hand your nametag is easy to read. During a handshake, the right shoulder moves in with the outstretched hand creating a line. The receiver's eyes follow the line and wearing your nametag on the right side helps the other person find it easily. *Right is Right.* If you are a longhaired woman (or man for that matter), be sure your hair does not cover your tag.

If you have a company nametag – wear it. This indicates that you are serious about your career and not just passing through this position on the way to becoming a hermit or something. No company nametag? Take a thick black marker to write your name on the name badge.

12. Carry /use breath mints or those dissolving strip things (not gum).
Halitosis is bad for business. Good breath is a must. And as for gum, smacking anything at a networking function is discouraged.

13. Beware of the "Mound o' Stuff."

At many networking functions put on by Chambers of Commerce and the like, it is common to be able to put a flyer or brochure on everyone's chair prior to the event. Often when participants get to their chair, there is literally half an inch of business cards, flyers, four-color brochures, Hershey's kisses, candy canes (during the holidays) and a hodgepodge of promotional knickknacks needing to be moved out of the way so they can sit down.

Putting something on everyone's chair can be worthwhile. It can also be a HUGE waste of time and money. Rest assured, every trash bin within a hundred-yard radius will be overflowing with this stuff after the event, and most people do not even take the time to dig through the chair-mound.

Why should they? What's in it for them?

If you put something on every chair, make it inexpensive, memorable, useful, or include a call to action – like a pen, a little calendar, or a special flyer featuring a really cool time-sensitive offer. No business cards or four-color brochures. A business card should be a personal hand-off presented via a face-to-face handshake. Those jazzy color brochures are way too expensive. *It is too much.*

If you have something worthwhile, make sure you get there early to distribute your items before participants start arriving. Nothing says "I do not have my stuff together" like trying to pass around your discount coupon after most people have already taken a seat.

Keep one of your items on hand and put the rest in your car or out of the way. When it is your time to do your "Rise and Shine" (addressed on pages 103-105), hold up the item and explain why it is worth their time to hunt through the mound for it.

Try a special drawing where you put a couple of dots on a couple of your flyers. Everyone has to look for your flyer to see if they have a dot. If they have one, they win something cool.

14. Respect the person's time.
Someone important to you is important to others. Strike up an engaging, unique conversation, learn something about them, make a solid impression, get their card, and excuse yourself at the appropriate moment. This will create a solid and classy first impression.

15. Pretend you are the host or hostess.
Introducing people you meet to others whom they may have something in common with earns big points. If you meet someone who is new to the event or a new member of the organization, answer their questions and then look around for someone who may be good for them to know. This keeps you moving and positions you as someone interested in helping others. When in doubt as to how a person wants to be introduced, use last names only.

16. Always keep it positive.

New Someone: *How are you?*
You: *I am great. How are you?*

New Someone: *How is business?*
You: *Rocking along. We're getting a lot of quality referrals.*

New Someone: *How do you like the weather?*
You: *Oh, I love rain.*

You get my point. Keep it positive. Do not be a whiner. Do not be an Eeyore or an Oscar the Grouch. No one wants to listen to complaining, fault-finding, or snooty attitudes.

17. Do not talk negatively about others *(especially competitors).*
Others are aware, if you speak badly to them about others behind
their back, that you may also speak poorly of them when they are
not around. Talking bad about competitors makes you look shallow
and weak, and puts the focus on them instead of you.

Plus, if you speak ill of someone, it will probably get back to them
and start some unhealthy and unprofitable competition.

18. Do NOT air dirty laundry in public.
I was at a networking function where a guy used his time in front of
the group to show us a three-ring binder he had created full of his
negative correspondence with a certain local business owner. It was
a major downer. Then he passed the three-ring binder around. This
created a really weird negative vibe and discouraged me from
wanting to build a real solid relationship with him. *What if he starts
three-ring binders on everybody?*

19. Communicate that your network rocks.
Talk enthusiastically about the cool, neat, highly productive and
witty people who are already in your network. This will encourage
others to want to be in your network too, because you will speak of
them in the same positive way.

20. Who wants a drink-e-poo?
At conferences, conventions, trade shows, and business-after-hours
functions *(often organized by the local Chamber of Commerce and
held at a local business establishment),* it is common for there to be
alcohol. I encourage you to consider not drinking at these events, or
at least know your alcohol limit and not get anywhere close to it.
Sure you want to be remembered, but not as the loud jerk who
couldn't hold his spirits and spilt red wine on Judge Jacob's new
power suit.

Asking Progress-Focused Questions

When meeting a new networking prospect, **do NOT hog the conversation and start talking about yourself, your business, how cool you are, or your ideal prospect.**

A much better choice is to invest the lion's share of the discussion asking questions about that person and their business. Find out what progress means to them.

> You make a much more powerful impression,
> a much more memorable impression,
> ***being interested in others***
> rather than trying to
> *be interesting to others.*

This should ease your mind and help you relax because now the pressure is off. All you have to do is work to answer these questions.

What is most important to that person at this moment?

What can I do to help this person progress?

Start by asking the person you are chatting with Who, What, Where, Why and How kinds of questions.

> **"The wise man is not the one**
> **who gives you the right answers,**
> **but the right questions."**
> *-- Claude Levi-Strauss*

People want and need to talk about THEIR business, NOT YOURS. That's cool – encourage them. It gets you valuable follow-up info and saves you from having to come up with something witty. Just listen and ask questions relating to what they say and people will think you ROCK. Always be thinking:

How can I help this person progress toward his or her goals?

Give direct eye contact and be totally focused on trying to get to know the other person better. People like to talk about how they got to where they are.

The more rapport you have with an individual, the more receptive they will be to establishing a relationship with you. Ask conversational questions that bring out the contact's uniqueness. Listen carefully and concentrate on what the person is saying. Get curious. It makes no sense to ask questions if you are not interested in the answers.

> **"The cure for boredom is curiosity.**
> **There is no cure for curiosity."**
> *-- Dorothy Parker*

Their answers should make it easier to make positive impressions in the future. People love to talk about themselves, so master the art of asking questions and listening to the responses so you can ask relevant questions. If you can help them with a tidbit of information or link them to a resource, you will be seen as a caring and knowledgeable person.

You can either make a suggestion related to what their needs are, or help them in some other way. The person will remember that you were able to help them out.

Plus you will gain knowledge. Knowledge is power, and asking questions is seeking that power. Asking people questions about themselves makes you stand out in their mind.

I have conducted countless interviews with business leaders and visionaries and have found that slight pauses before questions lead to longer answers. Taking these pauses show you are thinking and engaged, rather than just filling empty airtime.

It's okey-dokey to script your questions. Just rehearse them enough so they don't sound scripted.

Here are eight solid questions and statements for starting conversations and delivering solid first impressions:

1. *How did you get into your line of work?*

2. *What about the profession interested you?*

3. *What do you like most about your industry?*

4. *What major changes do you foresee in your industry?*

5. *What has been happening in your industry?*

6. *What are the current trends?*

7. *What have you found to be the best ways of getting the word out and promoting your business?*

8. *I'm meeting people all the time, tell me: How would I know if somebody I meet would be a good contact for you?*

> **"Good questions are far more difficult than good answers."**
> *-- Persian Proverb*

Also add these to your conversational Rolodex:

Tell me more.
Please elaborate.
What are your ideas about…?
There is something I would like to ask you…
What is your opinion on…?

Do not ask questions in rapid-fire succession. This is not a Dragnet interrogation or a time for cross-examination. Nor is it a time to relive your glory days on the debate team. Avoid asking questions that are manipulative, boring, embarrassing, hostile, confrontational, insulting, or too intimate.

When you approach people, they will start talking about something, so follow that with them and go with the flow. Abrupt changes in conversational course cause confusion and frustration.

Every question you ask makes a statement about you. Only ask questions that make you look good (smart, concerned, with-it, etc.).

Remember, it is going to take a series of progress-based impressions to go from *met* to *net*. Ask questions that help you with those future impressions. Ask questions that help you find the *next step* in building the relationship. The more you know about the person (their interests, their business, their needs, their likes, their family), the more ways you will have to *Be Progress* for them in the future. A major goal in connecting with someone that first time should be finding that next step.

Ask real questions. Get curious.

Find the next step. Be Progress ™.

Listening as if Your Lifestyle Depended on It. It Does!

Everyone has a need to talk and be heard. Treat others as if they are the most important people on the planet because – in their minds – they are. Everyone wants to feel that they are significant and have meaningful ideas to share. Those who choose to really listen will always have someone to talk with. Notice that I wrote talk <u>with</u>, not talk <u>to</u>. The key is to:

Turn people ON to you by tuning IN to them.

Good listeners absorb and reflect on what they hear. They are active in the listening process. This requires energy and motivation because listening is more than just hearing. We must become active listeners rather than passive hearers.

Often our motivation to actively listen is not all that high. We think we can get by without really focusing. This is a mistake. The ability to value what others say is critical to building priceless relationships. To make solid first impressions, be determined to understand completely what others are trying to communicate.

"No man ever listened himself out of a job."
-- Calvin Coolidge

Collect your thoughts and focus. Think only about the present conversation. How often do you catch yourself thinking about some unrelated issue when you should be listening? It is difficult to *tune in* when you're preoccupied with previous conversations or unfinished tasks.

Step 3: D – Deliver Solid First Impressions

Business philosopher Jim Rohn is quoted as saying, "One of the greatest gifts you can give anyone is the gift of your attention." *Rohn is right.* Don't get distracted by other people's nearby conversations. If you have to, walk the person you are speaking with to a quieter place in the room to have your initial chat.

Try this. Look directly at the person and when they stop speaking, count to two (in your mind!) before you speak.
Committing to this brief pause:
A. helps you avoid interrupting the other person, who may have only paused to gather his or her thoughts.
B. establishes that what has just been shared was worth contemplation.
C. gives your brain time to digest the information and ask a good clarifying question or make a comment.

Good clarifying questions offer the person the chance to rephrase their thoughts and say precisely what they mean. Repeating back (as questions or tentative statements) what you think you've heard the other person say also makes people feel wonderful, and it avoids mind-misreading errors.

If networking stresses you out, you may turn into an overanxious talker and end up overpowering the fine folks in the dialogue and not letting anyone else talk. Active listening can help prevent this from happening. Think about it:

In the past, at the end of a conversation, did you tend to know more about the person, or did they learn more about you?

Discipline yourself to uttering no more than four sentences in a row without stopping. This ensures that others will have the opportunity to express themselves.

Two ears, one mouth. You know the saying.

Insight on Business Cards and Note-taking

Do not focus on giving out business cards. Focus on receiving business cards and following up! Remember, it's not about walking out with twenty-five business cards; it's about engaging in quality conversations and getting the right business cards. Say something like: *May I have one of your cards so we can stay in touch?* Simple, huh?

If you begin a new quality relationship, then you have made progress and the event is a success. It is more imperative for you to learn something unique about the person, make a solid first impression, and acquire their card than for you to force a card into their pocket. They are just going to throw it away.

Whipping your card out on people right as you meet them makes you look needy, pushy, and somewhat desperate. Again, focus on making a solid connection, receiving their business cards, and following up by e-mail, snail mail, or phone within 24 hours. If they ask for your card, that is a bonus.

With that said, always have enough business cards. Carry them loose and handy in a pocket that is easily accessible. Have business cards with you at all times. You never know when someone may ask for one. Countless times I have encountered people at business functions who either didn't bring cards, ran out of cards, or did not even have cards. *Bad form.*

I carry a small notepad and pen in case the person I'm wanting to follow up with does not have a card. I write their contact info on the pad and there we go. Designate one pocket for incoming cards and one for your cards. Ladies, plan ahead and wear an outfit with a couple of pockets.

Take a pen because it's useful to write yourself *next-step reminders* on the back of the business cards you receive. You need this info to make your next progress-based impression. Plus, people like to see that they are worth your taking action. Write down stuff like where you met and things you talked about, but most important, **write what you are going to do to *Be Progress* for them.**

Later, study and go through the business cards collected. On the back of each, jot down more information. Note the date, event, topic of conversation, and the person's distinctive features: "cute and tall," "glasses," "deep voice," "Magnum P.I. mustache," etc.

Do yourself a favor and have a professional-looking business card. Your business card creates a mental image and reflects who you are, so make sure the card you are handing out:

- is easy to read.
- includes all the essential info (name, company, e-mail, phone #).
- clearly defines your business, service, and/or products.
- is printed on quality hard-stock paper. No straight-off-the-home-computer perforated cards. Nothing screams *"I am not totally committed to what I am doing"* like a flimsy perforated card.
- is YOUR card, not your manager's or coworker's, with their names crossed out and yours scribbled in.
- represents the business you are in today. Handing out cards and saying you are not there anymore, or having three different cards is confusing and not going to get positive buzz rolling your way.

Carry your business card with you to the grocery store, the mall, your Botox appointment, the gym, Chick-Fil-A, everywhere. You never know where your next client or customer will come from. Most people like to receive other people's cards during a face-to-face meeting, not have a stack of cards waiting for them as they are sitting down at a networking event. For the most part, business cards are hand-to-hand relationship tools.

The Rise and Shine:
Designing Your 30-Second Commercial

At many networking meetings, participants are given the opportunity to participate in what I call the **Rise and Shine**. This is usually a 30-second opportunity to *rise* from your chair and present yourself and what progress you offer through your business in a very concise, direct, and hopefully memorable way. This is your time to *shine*. You also benefit from hearing other participants give their promotional spot.

Do not use this time to brag. Egotism is boring. Focus on how you *help* others solve problems. *How are you providing progress?*

Here is a tried and true outline to follow:
My name is ___*(your name)*. I work with *(run)* a company called ____*(your company)*. We work with people *(organizations)* who are ready to ___ *(attract customers, get books in order, hire the right people, etc.)* so they can___ *(make more money, save time, be more productive, etc.)*, because everyone can use more ___*(money, time, productivity, etc.)*. ___ *(Your name)* with___ *(your company)*.

Important Related Tip:
Do not hold stuff in your hands when you do your Rise and Shine unless you are going to refer to it. It pulls focus away from you.

When meeting someone one-on-one, you have far less than the 30 seconds in a Rise and Shine to grab their attention. Come up with some progress-based statements that share your expertise and what you and your company offer in a clear, engaging way. If you talk aimlessly or just throw some stuff together on the fly, you may quickly lose their interest.

Always speak about what you do in a professional, positive manner. Concentrate on how others benefit from the product or service you perform.

It's important to communicate what you do in ways that will help the person you're speaking with understand that you provide solutions. They must have you positioned in their mind as an agent of progress.

Positioning revolves around quickly and clearly articulating who you work with, what problems you solve, what benefits you offer, and what results you produce. A solid way to relate this is to communicate a common problem, followed by the solution you provide. This approach works because most people are totally immersed in their own challenges 24/7.

Problem/Solution Example:
Debt Consolidator: *You know how a lot of people are drowning in debt and struggling to make ends meet? I offer a service that helps people gain control of their finances and their future.*

It is the benefit people want to hear about, not what you do. These statements need to become so automatic that you don't even think of them in terms of networking.

Stuff like:
I solve...
We save companies...
I help people...
We give ...
I make...
I teach the disorganized how to...
We design...

Avoid using your label as your introduction.
"I'm an insurance agent."
"I'm a car salesman."
"I'm an underwater basket-weaver."

Chances are, when you open with your label, if you get a continued conversation, that person is only being polite (well, not the underwater basket-weaver label – that sounds pretty interesting as is).

If you are a real estate agent: Say you assist people in finding their new Home Sweet Home.

If you are a financial advisor: Say you help people create wealth, financial independence, and peace of mind.

CPA: You do not do taxes. Heck, you're in the stress-reduction business.

If it fits your personality and service, it can be extremely profitable to come up with a hook or a catchy tag line that creates curiosity. These statements are memorable and start a conversation.

A great one that comes to mind is from Doug Trumbull, the owner of Mighty Clean Carpet Cleaners in Plano, Texas:
If it isn't Mighty Clean, it's a dirty shame.

Another good one I heard recently is from a pest-control company (specializing in getting rid of termites) in Providence, Rhode Island:
Without Griggs & Browne, the whole town would fall down.

Presence Power

How you hold your physical body communicates a tremendous amount of information about you. Be aware of presence power. Studies suggest that a person will unconsciously interpret approximately 55% of the meaning of your message from physiological cues from your attire, body position, stance, and facial expressions.

Body language, demeanor, and dress are important elements in making a lasting impression. First impressions are often lasting impressions. So take pride in your appearance. Be fun and sociable. You are the number-one element in your success strategy.

How you look and present yourself matters. You want to look smart and with-it. You should not look untidy. No messed up hair, wrinkled shirts, or loose ties. In fact, the ideal wardrobe for a networking event is slightly better dressed than the other attendees.

Check yourself before you go out. Do a 360 in front of a full-length mirror. *Would you want to talk to you? Would you want to be seen talking to you?*

Ask someone's opinion. Take the advice of others about your appearance. I ask my wife. She has saved me from more than a few bad shirt/tie combos.

However, do not rely on your "together" look to cover up for sad puppy behavior or poor conversational ability. Stand, speak, and act as if you were self-confident, attractive, vital. If you have *flair*, use it. Make sure you will be remembered in a positive way. Be enthusiastic. An enthusiastic attitude distinguishes the really *cracking* networkers from the *so-so* networkers.

Speak with a positive countenance, exhibit confidence, and display a natural enthusiasm about your life and your work. Be a walking-talking representation of life, in all its excitement and possibility. How you say something means as much or more than what you say. You are your best public relations representative. You are the person who knows best what you do and what you have to offer others.

Sit or stand up straight. Gesture with power and confidence. Be fully engaged. Nod in agreement. Smile. Do not fold your arms or let your eyes wander off into the distance; look like you are having a good time. People trust people who look them in the eye. Do not shift focus. The more you change your focus, the more new information your brain is taking in. If you change focus frequently, you can overload your brain to the point where you are "at sea" and unable to focus on the issue at hand.

Be careful about shifting your weight while chatting with someone. It communicates a lack of interest and confidence, and it can result in your contact feeling a lack of TRUST.

Also, do not keep your hands in your pockets the whole time and jingle-jangle-jingle your keys or change. *You are not there to provide musical backup or percussion for the event.*

Think about this:
Each positive first impression has the potential to turn into a priceless business relationship. People want to do business with professionals who are excited about life and who look like they have their act together.

Get Funny

Making someone laugh *(with you, not at you)* is definite progress. Humor attracts and holds attention. Many a person has walked away from a conversation out of sheer boredom. Make them laugh and they will like you. Humor can help make a great impression because it appeals to a person's need for pleasure and release.

Think I am just joking around? Humor has been scientifically proven to relieve stress, motivate, and improve relationships. The use of good humor relaxes people; in that state, they become more open. A tense or uncomfortable person is far less able or willing to have a good discussion with you.

> **"Laughter is the shortest distance between two people."**
> *-- Victor Borge*

Common sense is a prerequisite for using humor successfully. Avoid any attempt at political, sexual, or religious humor. Refrain from making off-color or derogatory remarks about others. Trying to get a chuckle at the expense of others shows a lack of professionalism, character, and good sense.

No jokes. Tell stories.
A joke is rarely original, memorable, or all that funny. (Of all the jokes you've been told in your life, how many do you remember?) They don't help the person you are talking to get to know you. Jokes make you look like you are trying too hard. They are contrived.

Jokes force your audience into the uncomfortable position of having to smile or chuckle when they're not amused. They act more as a shield than anything. Jokes are often risky because most are demeaning to some group of people. Stories are where it's at. They are genuine and offer a window into the real you.

The highest form of humor is to laugh at yourself; the lowest form is to laugh at someone else. Tell personal stories where the lesson is learned, or the embarrassment is suffered at your own expense. It will make you appear more vulnerable, approachable, and human. Poke fun at yourself and folks will laugh with you, not at you.

Don't be afraid of putting some egg on your own face early in the conversation. Self-deprecating humor is so effective that it is highly regarded as a leadership trait. It reflects confidence and strength. It shows that you are secure enough to laugh at yourself. It also creates instant rapport, defuses tension, and makes you more likable. Learn to laugh at what you do, without laughing at who you are.

Quick One Liner:
"I'm such a bad speller, my spell checker is stunned."

Tell stories that gently poke fun at yourself. Doing this acts as a social lubricant and shows that you are comfortable in your own skin and at ease with life. It encourages your listener to feel the same way. As early twentieth-century poet Ella Wheeler Wilcox wrote, "Laugh and the world laughs with you."

Rehearse your lines. In meeting people, we each have certain situations that seem to come up again and again. You can anticipate these situations and be ready with witty, fresh, well-rehearsed, "spontaneous" comebacks.

> **"There are three things that are real – God, human folly, and laughter. The first two are beyond comprehension. So we must do what we can with the third."**
> *-- John F. Kennedy*

Humor takes intelligence and subtle qualities like insight and sensitivity. Using humor displays a mastery of language and an openness to the human condition. If someone is "naturally funny," they are probably really intelligent. *Heck, ask them.*

Say: "Wow, you are FUNNY. What's your IQ?"
(Just messing.)

Study humor. Appreciate humor. Seek it out.
What was so funny? Why did you laugh?
Why did you not laugh? Why did you groan?

People are often envious of those who are funny and able to make others laugh. *I know I am envious of Jack Black, Dennis Miller's rants, early Steve Martin, and Bill Cosby, circa 1966. Cosby's comedy album "Wonderfulness" from that year is pure comedy gold.* Anyone can learn to be more humorous with a little practice. Humor is a technique that can be learned, developed, and perfected just like origami *(OK, not like origami, but you get the idea).*

Incorporate humor into your daily life. Once you cultivate humor, you have the foundation for intellectual rapport. Not every attempt will get a knee-slapping belly laugh; your mission is bigger than that. A comedian succeeds just by being funny, but a networker succeeds only when the humor helps to create a positive impression. But of course, humor will never substitute for solid listening skills. Mix too much yuck-yuck with too little care or respect and you will plummet, crash, and burn.

Some people will not even desire or enjoy humor. It will not take a rocket scientist to spot these folks because they will be the cats that won't chuckle at anything. The best thing to do in this scenario is to play it straight. Cut the humor and ask another open-ended question that gets them talking. Remember, the goal is to deliver a solid first impression. You are not auditioning for a gig on Leno.

Adapting Your Style to Deliver Solid First Impressions

We each have our own style, our own way we like to communicate with others *(different strokes for different folks)*. This is a basic human fact. Each interaction with other people requires you to assess the situation from a fresh perspective.

It is also a fact that we need to *connect* when we meet someone. Unfortunately, a tremendous amount of human energy is used unproductively in talking past or "at" each other. We often fail to make a real connection with someone because we have a set of behavioral preferences that do not mesh with those of the person on the other side of our bifocals.

Progress agents committed to cracking the networking CODE can utilize a keen awareness of individual behavioral differences and, without being chameleons, modify their own preferences to make a favorable impression.

Even though we are all unique, most people do fit into a certain style or predictable pattern of behavior. People with similar styles tend to exhibit specific types of behavior common to that style. Such patterns of behavior influence how people prefer to communicate and interact.

> **"Behavior is the mirror in which everyone shows their image."**
> *-- Johann Wolfgang von Goethe*

We need to strive to understand and embrace these different behavioral styles. This makes us better able to interact with other folks, even those who appear to be very different and sometimes

113

hard to understand. When we identify the behavioral differences in ourselves and others, we can adapt our style to create a comfortable environment for the person we are speaking with.

A solid understanding of the DISC behavioral model is useful for delivering solid first impressions. DISC measures observable behavior and emotions. The development of the DISC model is based on the work of American psychologist Dr. William Marston, an expert in behavioral styles.

In 1926, Marston published *The Emotions of Normal People,* in which he grouped people along two lines: either active or passive tendencies relative to their favorable or unfavorable view of the environment and their relationship to that environment.

Say what? Here is a view of DISC from 30,000 feet:

Some people are *Reserved* and some are *Outgoing*.
One type is not better than the other.

Some people are *People-Oriented* and some are *Task-Oriented*.
One type is not better than the other.

Each of us is a unique blend of:
Reserved or Outgoing, mixed with the quality of being People-Focused or Task-Focused.

Marston's DISC research showed how behavioral characteristics may be grouped into four fundamental styles (D.I.S.C.):

Dominance
Influence
Steadiness
Conscientiousness

D - Dominance

These are the Task-Oriented, Outgoing Types.

These folks are direct, demanding, determined, and decisive.
They are confident, competitive, take-action doers.
They will likely ask WHAT questions more than HOW questions.

Some famous dominant behavior types are:
Donald Trump, Margaret Thatcher, Henry Ford, General Patton, Mark Cuban, Barbara Walters, Vince Lombardi.

To deliver a solid first impression to D-types:
Be concise and direct. These people need prestige, authority, and control.

I - Influence

These are the People-Oriented, Outgoing Types.

These folks are interactive, inspirational, impressive, and interested in people. They are friendly, outgoing, emotional "talkers."
They will likely ask WHO questions more than WHY questions.

Some famous influential behavior types are:
Oprah Winfrey, Will Farrell, Bill Cosby, Sally Field (You like me. You really like me!), George Lopez, Bill Clinton, Wayne Brady.

To deliver a solid first impression to I-types:
Skip the details, socialize, and show excitement.
These people need recognition, acceptance, and to be heard.

S - Steadiness

These are the Reserved, People-Oriented Types.

These folks are stable, sensitive, and supportive. They are loyal, dependable, and good listeners. They will likely ask HOW questions more than WHAT questions.

Some famous steady behavior types are:
Mister Rogers, Mother Teresa, Albert Schweitzer, Florence Nightingale, Mahatma Gandhi, Tonto (The Lone Ranger's faithful Indian companion).

To deliver a solid first impression to S-types:
Be reassuring and take it slow. These people need security, appreciation, and time to decide if there should be a relationship.

C - Conscientiousness

These are the Reserved, Task-Oriented Types.

These folks are competent, careful, calculating, contemplative, and cautious. They are analytical, detailed, and do not show emotions readily. They will likely ask WHY questions more than WHO questions.

Some famous conscientious behavior types are:
Emily Post, Tom Landry, Isaac Newton, Columbo (OK, not a real dude, but you get the point), Johann Sebastian Bach, Michelangelo, Sherlock Holmes (again, not a real guy).

To deliver a solid first impression to C-types:
Be prepared and structured. These people need facts and are committed to quality.

116

Of course, all typologies are approximations. People display varying amounts of these four dimensions rather than just one. However, understanding the four different behavioral styles makes us better able to make positive impressions, even with those who we see as "different" or hard to understand. Being sensitive to these differences creates a relaxed environment where people want to move the relationship forward and offer their best.

> **"Behave so the aroma of your actions may enhance the general sweetness of the atmosphere."**
> *-- Henry David Thoreau*
> *(OK, that quote was a stretch. But every book like this gotta have a little Thoreau.)*

Recognize and respect individual nuances, make adjustments, use good judgment, and adapt. Learning and incorporating the DISC model of behavior is valuable for increasing trust and keeping communication open.

In my work with individuals and within organizations, I have had the opportunity to research and utilize several useful educational tools based on the DISC model. Feel free to contact me for further information.

A few interesting side notes:

Much later in his life, Dr. Marston created "Wonder Woman" while serving as an educational consultant for DC Comics. Authoring the Wonder Woman comic, Marston used a pen name: Charles Moulton.

The desire to understand the reasons for our diverse behavior has been an age-old preoccupation. *The explanations of the ancients were interesting:*

Empedocles (444 B.C.), the founder of a school of medicine in Sicily, believed that everything is made of earth, air, fire, and water. These external elements combine in an infinite number of ways, thus explaining the diversity of behavior.

In 400 B.C. the Greek physician Hippocrates came to the conclusion that it is not external factors that shape behavior. He disagreed with many of his day who believed human behavior was determined by being born under a certain astrological configuration of planets. Hippocrates theorized that it was something that takes place "inside" the individual.

Hippocrates believed that if people had a fast, hot fluid running inside their body, they would be direct, decisive, and a leadership-type person. If one had a fluid that was warm and slow, that person would be family- and relationship-oriented.

Even though Hippocrates' 'blood theory' didn't hold much water, it was the first substantial method for identifying and grouping types of human behavior.

Step 4

E - Earn Trust

Trust Makes Money

The final step to *Cracking the Networking CODE* is to:
Earn Trust.

You may not believe this, but meeting people and making a solid first impression is the easy part. Earning their trust is hard. Earning their trust takes a series of Progress-based Impressions.

So keep it up. Keep on keeping on being progress. Keep making great impressions. This is why getting to know people and their interests during the first conversation is so important. The more you know about them – their lives, their goals – the more ways you can help them progress and earn their trust.

As Captain D. Michael Abrashoff, former commander of the *USS Benfold*, relates in his book, *It's Your Ship*, **Trust makes money.** Trust is the basis for profitable long-term relationships. Building trust takes time. Trust is the promise of progress.

Trust is fragile and can be weakened by broken promises and unrealistic expectations. So mean what you say and do what you say you will do.

The power in building relationships comes from what you know about who you know, and how you creatively use that knowledge. The more you know about someone in your network, the more ways you can be progress for his or her life.

What are they going for in life?
What do they like?
What are their interests?

Find ways to help them progress based on their needs – not on your services. People want to be in relationships with people who bring progress into their lives. They trust people who continually bring progress into their lives.

My definition of trust is 'the promise of progress.' People must trust that you care and offer value.   There must be benefits gained from being in a relationship with you, or there will be no relationship.

As relationships blossom, continue to look for ways to establish yourself as a *Progress Agent* ™ in their lives.

The Six Ps of Progress:

Pleasure
Peace of Mind
Profit
Prestige
Pain Avoidance
Power™

The 24-Hour Follow-up

Get that second progress-based impression in quick.
Follow up by e-mail, snail mail, or phone within 24 hours. You want to get the second progress-based impression in quick to build on the momentum of the first. The longer you wait, the harder it is and the more likelihood that the buzz of meeting you will have waned. It is vital that you include in your follow-up something specific to the initial conversation you had with the contact.

Most people do not follow up because they have nothing to say that builds on the conversation – ***because there was no real conversation!*** They did not learn anything that they can use to build on. *They did not find the next step.* A good fast follow-up that builds on the first conversation and offers progress sets you apart from the rest. It is strategic communication that begins to solidify your relationship.

Here are the three major follow-up methods for solid progress-based second impressions:

The Follow-up Phone Call
Making follow-up phone calls is good, but you will probably end up in voice mail. When you do (and you will), start and end your message with your name and phone number. If you are given the opportunity to listen to your voice message and redo it, take it.

Say your name and number slowly and distinctly, without "swallowing" any words or syllables. Assume that the person listening remembers you, enjoyed your time together, and wants to write your number down and get in contact with you. Include a compliment or a statement that refers back to the conversation you shared.

The Follow-up E-mail
There is no doubt that e-mail is a powerful, inexpensive, and widely used means of communication today. I like e-mail. It provides you with access that the phone and snail mail do not. The same people who ignore phone messages may well respond to e-mail. The secret is to create e-mails that are personal and focus on the relationship you have started with them – not on what your company does.

> **"Make yourself necessary to the world and mankind will give you bread."**
> -- *Ralph Waldo Emerson*

The subject line of your e-mails needs to encourage the receiver to open it. Create a signature file that includes your full name, e-mail address, and phone number so it will be easy for them to contact you. Include in your signature file a brief but powerful statement of how you empower progress.

And make sure all your e-mails include the address to your own or your company's Web site.

Don't have one?
Get one, a good one.

People often will check out your Web site just because you make it easy for them by including it in your correspondence. Most people are curious and your Web presence can serve as another positive impression that builds trust.

Your Web site must have up-to-date info, be attractive and easy to navigate, and be chock-full of testimonials from your thrilled customers and clients.

The Follow-up Note
Sending a follow-up note is a solid way to build a new relationship. Short, upbeat, and handwritten would be ideal (as long as your writing is legible!). It would also be ideal to send one to everyone you meet *(tough to pull off, but ideal).*

Again, begin with a compliment or a statement that refers back to the conversation you shared. Keep the tone upbeat and end by suggesting that the two of you get together for breakfast or lunch.

Many feel that a follow-up written thank-you note is better than a follow-up e-mail. A real signature in ink on real notepaper may take a couple of days to get to them, but it has the potential of being much more memorable than an e-mail.

To meet the 24-hour follow-up timeline, try taking some thank-you stationery or note cards with stamps to networking events. Write, address, and mail the notes directly following the event to the people you just met.

10 Ideas for Creating a Series of Progress-Based Impressions

Don't quit now. Keep the progress coming. Follow through. Remember, it takes a series of progress-based impressions to earn trust and go from *met* to *net*.

> **"When you get right down to the root**
> **of the meaning of the word** *succeed*,
> **you find it simply means**
> *to follow through."*
> *-- F. W. Nichol*

Here are ten solid ideas for creating a series of progress-based impressions:

1. Document and track all your networking contacts.
As soon as you can, put each of your new contacts into your database, detail your notes, and plan your *next step* with each of them. Structure your communication in a way that engages the other person and draws their interest.

2. Reconnect at functions.
When you see someone in your network at an event, take a moment to put in a *quick "How's it going?"* It's energizing to connect with your network, and a little maintenance goes a long way.

> **"Enjoy yourself. If you can't enjoy yourself,**
> **enjoy somebody else."**
> *-- Jack Schaefer*

If you run into someone whose name you have forgotten, it is not *bad* to ask for their name again, but try to remember it for the next time your paths cross. *Two strikes and you're out.*

3. Send thank-you notes to everyone who helps you.
Anyone who gives you a lead, valuable information, or a referral
gets a thank-you note *(or at least a thank you e-mail)*. Keep them
informed of the progress you're making because of their help.
It makes them feel useful and important, and who doesn't like that?
Encouraging and rewarding your net strengthens your net.

4. Look for something to acknowledge people for.
Genuinely complimenting someone costs you nothing, but to the
recipient, a heartfelt compliment and the feelings it generates cannot
be bought at any price. Recognition, encouraging words, and pats
on the back are all excellent ways of making positive impressions,
especially if done in front of others.

Avoid general compliments as they may just seem like flattery,
"sucking up." Much more powerful is a comment about something
positive that person has done: compliment on behavior or
achievements.

> **"Kind words can be short and easy to speak,**
> **but their echoes are truly endless."**
> *-- Mother Teresa*

A thoughtful person is a remembered person. Be generous of spirit.
You will get back much more than what you put out. The end result
of acknowledging and praising others is that you have given people
reasons to speak well of you to others. Such word-of-mouth
character endorsements are far more powerful than anything you
could ever say about yourself.

It does not matter how successful a person is, or how good that
person feels inside: it is always nice to know that others appreciate
one's personality, talent, uniqueness, attitude, or accomplishments.
You can compliment someone about any one of hundreds of things.
Just keep it real and don't go overboard. Insincerity can be sensed.

5. Be a "Hub of Information."

Never miss a chance to offer contacts a referral to important people, organizations, information, and opportunities. Be a valuable person for someone to build a relationship with. Work at it. If you focus on giving information and support rather than cultivating contacts for your own benefit, your network will grow naturally. Make it easy for others to see that you are in their corner. Help them feel cared about and important.

Make information flow in and out of your life. Work to be known as someone who has great information and contacts and is willing to share them. Work to be known as a Progress Agent ™. Always be poised to make a referral for someone else. It will all come back around. When you learn something new, ask yourself:

Who in my network would find this information valuable?

Share it (as long as it isn't confidential). When reading an article, always ask yourself:

Who in my network would be helped by this article?

Forward useful articles via e-mail, or send clippings from newspapers or magazines that relate to or affect the people in your network. If you mail an article, keep in mind that the real article is better than a photocopy of it. Simply clip it out, attach your card with an FYI Post-it, and drop it in the mail.

If the person you're chatting with is having a challenge with bookkeeping, offer to e-mail the number of a couple of good CPAs. Be a resource for people and they will become a resource for you. Turn them on to useful business books. Learn about the other person's profession and, if it feels right, offer to call a contact on their behalf. To get referrals, give referrals. If you give without keeping track, you get repaid without ever asking for it.

Help others first. Offer your information with no strings attached. Connect people and position yourself as a resource to others on a totally altruistic basis. Favors with strings attached are not favors and not nearly as appreciated.

6. Keep in touch with people.
People move on, over, and up more than ever before. In an ideal scenario, we would have built a network and kept good track of it early in our careers. If you are just starting out, I encourage you to do just that. But it's never too late to begin. Keep in touch with people. Keep track of them.

Figure out the best ways to get back in touch with people who have not heard from you in a while. Pick up the phone and call them. Stay tight with them. The longer you wait to call somebody, the harder it is. Work to strengthen the relationship by offering them your information, friendship, and help. Do not contact others only when you want something. Bad form, and people are sure to notice.

7. Publish a newsletter via e-mail.
Create and distribute a newsletter via e-mail to inspire still more positive impressions. The newsletter needs to provide great info and stuff that your readers will appreciate. Make sure they want your newsletter. Do not spam them! Ask if they would like a free subscription. I think my team puts out a good one. If you would like to check out our e-mail-based newsletter, **The Progress Report**, you can subscribe at: www.ProgressAgents.com. It's free.

Once you have started an e-mail newsletter – STICK WITH IT. Sending it out every now and then will not deliver as powerful a message as being consistent with it. We have chosen to publish ours twice a month. Sometimes that is tough to pull off. We are committed because we have experienced firsthand the power of consistency. Plus, once I get going, I dig writing. Sometimes I do not know when to stop. And I just keep writing and writing and …

8. Use a cartoon filing system.
If it fits your personality and services, clip cartoons with people's names in them. For example, you might look out for a cartoon with "Steve" in it. Whenever you find a cartoon with a name in it, file it. Once a month, get out your contact database and your file folder full of cartoons. Match the cartoons to contacts' names and send off five to ten personal notes, each with a cartoon and a business card. Also clip cartoons that relate to a person's interests, hobbies, or pets. If you find out that someone owns a bulldog, be on the lookout for a cartoon featuring a bulldog.

A couple of words of caution:
Make sure that your contact appreciates the gesture. Some people don't like to be "bothered" with amusing mail. Also, be careful that the humor in the cartoon doesn't offend the contact.

9. Celebrate with them by sending cards
and small thoughtful gifts.
Send cards celebrating your contacts' birthdays, promotions, graduations, and anniversaries. Listen intently and notice if your contact expresses a particular interest in something that could be turned into a gift. If so, make a note, and on the person's next birthday you can personally present or send them the perfect gift.

10. Challenge yourself.
At the start of each day, or as you plan for the next day, jot down the names of three to five people you are going to reconnect with during that business day. Develop the habit of contacting at least one person every week who you haven't had a good chat with in a while. Meet them for breakfast, for lunch, or for drinks after work. Whatever you're doing to stay in touch, challenge yourself to do a little more. Stay in touch with your network to keep it alive and active.

Keep making positive impressions. Keep earning trust.

Get a Mentor

To keep yourself on track and consistently offering progress and earning trust, seek out a mentor. Mentors help you see beyond your present vision by providing practical advice, ideas, and valuable concepts based on their unique experience and the wisdom gained from their failures, as well as their successes. They can play a significant role in the life of a successful networker. A person you respect can guide you and share their wisdom without reservation.

Make a list of people you believe can impact your networking success.

Who has earned your trust?

Find a way to connect with these people today. Mentors should be role models of the kind of person you are working to become. Be sure to get your advice from the veterans who have "been there, done that" and who sport the "I feel successful" T-shirt.

A mentor can:

– guide you in crafting networking goals.
– make you accountable.
– show you how to network
  (not just tell you or toss you an extremely well-put-together book on networking, like the one in your hands).
– encourage you to network often.
– offer you feedback and help you identify and overcome obstacles to your networking success.
– share in celebrating your success.
– dissect and analyze your setbacks.

Why would they want to mentor you?

Most successful people had mentors and recognize how important those mentors were in their development. They are "Paying It Forward" *(great concept, OK movie)*. Others are at the place in their career where they want to give back. They like you, trust you, and choose to help you because it would bring them pleasure to see you succeed.

> **"Asking for help does not mean that we are weak or incompetent. It usually indicates an advanced level of honesty and intelligence."**
> *-- Anne Wilson Schaef*

Look for someone who:
– listens to others and displays good communication skills.
– demonstrates integrity and enthusiasm for their life and career.
– models continuous improvement and the importance of networking.
– shares their mistakes and how they grew from these learning experiences.
– seeks opportunities for personal and professional growth.
– stays informed by reading and attending seminars.

Use these high achievers wisely. Do not mishandle the privilege and start whining about how tough things are out there. With this privilege comes responsibility. You must bring value to the alliance. If you start believing your short-term objectives are more important than your long-term relationships, you will betray the trust and do more harm than good. Acknowledge your mentors as you progress. Something as simple as a sincere thank-you and a pat on the back can serve as their inspiration to continue being there for you.

Continue to earn their trust.

Get Cracking!

Do not get stuck in the "Woulda, Coulda, Shoulda" Trap. Solid networking skills are good to possess but they are only useful if you USE them. Don't just *plan* to network. Reach out! Networking takes personal self-discipline and dedication. Every day, hundreds of thousands of people have hundreds of thousands of ideas, goals, and intentions – but they never take that first step.

Hey, you've known networking was a good business practice for a while now. *So why have you not done more of it up to this point?* One of the main reasons people don't take the first step is they have little vision of the outcome they're looking for through networking. They're not clear on why it's worth the trouble of finding the events, getting dressed up, and making themselves stressed out and uncomfortable.

Increase your determination to make networking work for you by listing the reasons you haven't done more in the past. Getting to the bottom of your resistances will encourage you to blast through them – *by just doing it.* And once you get on a roll, you won't stop. It could even become second nature to you.

Want a way to get really motivated to keep networking? You do? OK. Try this:

Create a Cracking the CODE Connection Map
Create a visual representation of your NET. Make it just like a family tree, except have this one show how each of your new contacts leads to others. You can easily keep track of your progress. And when you see how networking has helped, you'll be more motivated to keep making new contacts and developing your network.

Work to move beyond your shyness and take full advantage of all the networking opportunities that come your way.

Wait. Strike that. Do not just take advantage of the networking opportunities that come your way. **PROACTIVELY MAKE OPPORTUNITIES** to broaden your net.

Networking is one part social skills and one part sales skills, mixed with a couple shots of life skills. Networking is as natural as breathing. We all do it all the time. Whenever you ask someone's opinion to help you make an informed decision, even if it is just to find a good sushi bar or a DVD at Blockbuster, you are reaping the benefits of networking. Gathering new contacts and opening avenues of opportunity increases the number of people in your network.

Get out more often. Attend more general business events and industry functions. If you don't meet new people, your network will shrink, stagnate, and lose its strength.

Yes, most of these events happen in the mornings, during lunches, and after hours. Look, success is rarely created working 9 to 5. What a way to make a livin'. It is all takin' and no givin'. *Thank you, Dolly Parton.*

Networking is not about chance meetings. *Hard work* makes luck, my friend. Go make some luck. I know that sometimes a business luncheon may seem like a waste of time, especially if all you do is eat and make random chit chat. But it will not feel like that when you learn how to effectively network at these events. Even if your BlackBerry or ACT database system is bursting with names, numbers, and e-mail addresses, it will not do you a bit of good unless you build the relationships.

Be a success in your own mind.
Be optimistic. Expect the best.
Get PHAT. Create an aura of inevitability.
Display a great attractive attitude.
(This just in: Your attitude counts for more than your knowledge.)
Harness the power of the Six Ps of Progress™.
Get out and about.
Listen. Be interested.
Ask great questions. Get curious.
Give a hoot.
Find the next step.
Be helpful.
Get involved. Stay in touch.
Become a Progress Agent™.

Sure, being in business is challenging.
Sure, it's nerve-racking to look for a new job.
Sure, sales can be tough to come by.
Sure, marketing is a moving bull's-eye.
Sure, people are often pressed for time.

But here is something else I know for sure: People do business with, as well as help, share information, brainstorm, and give referrals to people they trust and value. They trust and value people who genuinely care about them and are progress for their lives. They trust and value people who offer the *promise of progress*.

Create personal curb appeal.
Open face-to-face relationships.
Deliver solid first impressions.
Earn trust.

Be Progress™. Crack the Networking CODE.

Come on. Jump in. The water's fine.

Index

face-to-face relationships.
　　　See Opening face-to-face relationships
False Evidence Appearing Real, 48
Farrell, Will, 115
Fast Company, 56
fear, conquering, 47–51
Field, Sally, 115
first impressions.
　　　See Delivering solid first impressions
following up
　　in earning trust, 123–125, 131
　　in solid first impressions, 101, 102
　　with trade show contacts, 76
food. *See also* eating right
　　hanging out near, 80
　　not eating, 73, 75
Footloose, 45
Ford, Henry, 53, 115
Fortune, 56
Franken, Al, 53
Freeman, Morgan, 45
friends. *See also* relationships
　　gatekeepers as, 82–83
　　as networking benefit, 21
　　at networking events, 77, 79
　　as networking source, 83

Gandhi, Mahatma, 116
gatekeepers, forming relationships with, 82–83
Gates, Bill, 36
Getting Rich Your Own Way (Tracy), 56
gift giving, 131
giving a hoot, 33, 137
giving attention, 100. *See also* listening
giving before receiving, 28
goals, for networking events, 62, 64.
　　　See also planning
God, 56
golf, as networking tool, 70
Google, 36, 55
Grava, Andra, 41
Greenspan, Alan, 49
Griggs & Browne, 105
Grove, Andrew S., 21
Guerrilla Marketing (Levinson), 56
gum chewing, 90

halitosis, 73, 90
handouts, 89, 91–92
handshakes, 89
Hippocrates, 118
hobbies, organizations based on, 70
Holmes, Sherlock, 116
hoot, giving a, 33, 137
Hot Springs, Arkansas, 15–16
How to Win Friends and Influence People
　　(Carnegie), 56
humor
　　benefits of using, 109–111
　　in cartoon mailings, 131
　　inappropriate, 75, 109

impressions.
　　　See Delivering solid first impressions;
positive impressions
Influence style, 115
information, as networking benefit, 21
introductions. *See also* referrals
　　advantages of making, 92
　　in defining networking plan, 64
　　to finish conversations, 90
　　and handshakes, 89
　　as networking benefit, 21
　　tips for getting and giving, 78
　　using labels in, 105
It's Your Ship (Abrashoff), 56, 121

Jagger, Mick, 36
Jordan, Michael, 42
journals, reading, 56. *See also* newsletters

keeping in touch, 130, 131, 137
Kennedy, John F., 110
King, Martin Luther, Jr., 42
Kristofferson, Kris, 45

labels, in introductions, 105
Lachey, Nick, 36
Lake Hamilton (Arkansas), 15–16
Lake Ouachita (Arkansas), 15–16
Landry, Tom, 116
laughter, 109, 110. *See also* humor
leads groups, 71
Lebowitz, Fran, 57

About the Author

Recognized as a *"sales-and-networking guru"* by the *Dallas Business Journal,* Dean Lindsay is the founder of The Progress Agents LLC – a workshop and seminar company dedicated to empowering progress in sales, service, and workplace performance. Clients range from Fortune 100 companies to budding entrepreneurs, and from national and state associations to successful small businesses on both sides of the Atlantic.

Dean writes the column **Be Progress** ™ for various business publications and is a featured contributor to the nationally distributed audio publication *Selling Power Live.* He is also the head writer and editor of the widely read e-mail-based newsletter, **The Progress Report**.

A cum laude graduate of the University of North Texas, Dean presently serves on the Executive Advisory Board for UNT's Department of Marketing and Logistics. In June of 2005, the *Dallas Business Journal* selected Mr. Lindsay as one of Dallas/Ft.Worth's Rising Stars Under Age Forty in The Business World Today in their yearly **Forty Under 40** list.

Dean's unique knack for communicating and his commitment to helping people take positive steps make him a *Progress Agent*™. His speaking and consulting style is refreshingly daring, imaginative, and a lot of fun.

Dean is an avid runner and has completed the Stockholm Marathon in Stockholm, Sweden, and the Motorola Marathon in Austin, Texas. He lives in a suburb of Dallas, Texas, with his wife Lena and their two strong and wonderfully nutty daughters, Sofia and Ella.

Questions and Comments on *Cracking the Networking CODE* are encouraged and may be sent to:
Dean@ProgressAgents.com
1-877-479-5323
Really – contact him.
He would be jazzed to hear from you.

Want a subscription to The Progress Report ?

(It's FREE.)

Log on to www.ProgressAgents.com today.

Here is what subscribers say about The Progress Report.

"I get excited every time I see **The Progress Report** in my in-box. There is always something motivational and/or instructional that makes a bright spot in my day. Thanks for the tips, quotes, reminders, and overall great support! You have helped me to be more successful and keep my focus in the right direction! You help me to BE PROGRESS! Thank you so much for providing a great resource!"

-- Roxanne Lowry
Manager, Business Development
American Express

"Dean's personal energy explodes from my PC each month when I open his latest **Progress Report**. Reading Dean's articles is like having him in the room with you – his wit and insight get right to the point, and the point is always right on. His recent article on the Seven Time-Management Tips for Progress Agents put a realistic 'spin' on things I can do to manage my biggest challenge!"

-- Linda Boyle
Learning & Development
Homecomings Financial

"Dean's **Progress Report** comes to me via e-mail and proceeds to jump-start me for the rest of the month. It's a quick read with do-it-now information that makes sense!"

-- Cindy Peters, CRS
Business Development
Republic Title Company

"A quick read, **The Progress Report** is a great tool for staying focused on doing what's important now. It's like having a sales managers' meeting in a box. From resources to research to training tips, it's invaluable."

-- Maria Elena Duron
Founder and President
The Duromar Group

"I really have enjoyed receiving **The Progress Report**. Dean has the ability to transmit his upbeat personality and positive view of life into words. It truly comes through. I'm always looking for a new catchphrase or a spin on something I do routinely, and often find it in **The Progress Report**. Keep it coming."

-- Ed Brady,
President, Metrocrest Chamber of Commerce

"I really enjoy **The Progress Report**! It is chock-full of practical tips on sales, service, and motivation. Unlike some other e-zines I receive, I truly look forward to getting yours. I can read it in a few minutes and still gain tremendous value. I also love your final quote. So much can be learned from others' wisdom. Thanks for sharing yours! Keep up the great work!"

-- Patrick Donadio, MBA
Certified Speaking Professional (CSP)
Master Certified Coach (MCC)

"**The Progress Report** is a hip digest of tips that remind me to constantly 'sharpen my saw.' It never fails; there's a great nugget in every issue I can add to my repertoire of business-building techniques. Thanks, Dean!"

-- Jeff Moses
Owner, The Marketing Department

Subscribe Today.
www.ProgressAgents.com

Dean Lindsay is available for consulting projects, seminars, training, and keynote presentations to groups of all sizes.

"Dean is one of the best speakers I have ever seen: engaging, persuasive, and passionate."

> *-- Amy Dunker*
> *Vice President Business Development*
> *Western Union*

"Dean's ideas work. I have encouraged several professionals needing a boost in their bottom lines to retain the superior consulting services of Dean Lindsay and I encourage you to as well."

> *-- Michael Whitehead*
> *President, Whitehead and Mueller*
> *Environmental & Engineering Consulting Services*

"Dean's presentation style is world class: entertaining, inviting, enlightening, and dynamic."

> *-- Michael Bellomy*
> *General Manager*
> *SBC Communications*

"Dean rivets you to the topic. He is a must see."

> *-- Kelley Akins*
> *Sales Professional*
> *Pacific Life & Annuity*

"Dean's program was the perfect fit and one of the best we have ever had."

> *-- Judi Phares*
> *President and Founder*
> *RTI/Community Management Associates, Inc.*

See other side for Dean Lindsay's most requested keynotes and seminar topics.

Most Requested Keynote, Workshop, and Seminar Topics:

Cracking the Networking CODE
4 Steps to Priceless Business Relationships

The Making of a Progress Agent™
Be Progress™. Have a Big PHAT Day!

Cherishing Customers
Customer Relationships on the MEND

Diving for Referral Pearls
Cultivating Quality Referrals

ZONE Selling
Four Keys to Sales Success

Presence Power
Perfecting Presentation Performance

To schedule Dean for your next event or for information
on the full range of programs and services of Dean Lindsay
and The Progress Agents, contact your favorite speakers bureau,
log on to: www.ProgressAgents.com, or call 1-877-479-5323.

To discuss a consulting project, e-mail Dean Lindsay directly at
dean@ProgressAgents.com

For the latest information on *Cracking the Networking CODE*
audio and video products as well as other educational tools designed
by Dean Lindsay and The Progress Agents to
empower progress in sales, service, and workplace performance:

Log on to www.ProgressAgents.com
Call The Progress Agents toll free at: 1-877-479-5323

*All products are available at special quantity discounts
for sales promotions, premiums, fundraising,
or educational uses.*

Cracking the Networking CODE Order Form

*Give the Gift of Priceless Business Relationships
to all those in your network.*

CHECK YOUR LEADING BOOKSTORE OR ORDER HERE.

☐ Yes, I want ___ copies of *Cracking the Networking CODE* at $15.95 each, plus $4 shipping per book (Texas residents please add $1.32 sales tax per book). Allow 15 days for delivery.

☐ My check or money order for $ _____ is enclosed.

Please charge my ☐ Visa ☐ MasterCard ☐ Discover
☐ American Express

International orders must be paid by credit card or accompanied by a postal money order in U.S. funds. Please add $6 shipping per book.

Name _____
Organization _____
Address _____
City/State/Zip _____
Phone _____ E-mail _____
Card # _____ Exp. Date _____
Signature _____

Would you like a free subscription to *The Progress Report* ? Yes☐

Please make check or money order payable to:

7801 Alma, Suite 105-323
Plano, TX 75025-3483

Order online at:

WWW.WORLDGUMBO.COM

Order by phone at: 1-888-318-2911